The Role of Commu
Extremism

Conflict

August John Hoffman
Saul Alamilla • Belle Liang

The Role of Community Development in Reducing Extremism and Ethnic Conflict

The Evolution of Human Contact

palgrave
macmillan

HUMBER LIBRARIES LAKESHORE CAMPUS
3199 Lakeshore Blvd West
TORONTO, ON.   M8V 1K8

August John Hoffman
Metropolitan State University
Hudson, WI, USA

Saul Alamilla
Kennesaw State University
Kennesaw, GA, USA

Belle Liang
Boston College
Chestnut Hill, MA, USA

ISBN 978-3-030-09302-0   ISBN 978-3-319-75699-8   (eBook)
https://doi.org/10.1007/978-3-319-75699-8

© The Editor(s) (if applicable) and The Author(s) 2018
Softcover re-print of the Hardcover 1st edition 2018
This work is subject to copyright. All rights are solely and exclusively licensed by the Publisher, whether the whole or part of the material is concerned, specifically the rights of translation, reprinting, reuse of illustrations, recitation, broadcasting, reproduction on microfilms or in any other physical way, and transmission or information storage and retrieval, electronic adaptation, computer software, or by similar or dissimilar methodology now known or hereafter developed.
The use of general descriptive names, registered names, trademarks, service marks, etc. in this publication does not imply, even in the absence of a specific statement, that such names are exempt from the relevant protective laws and regulations and therefore free for general use. The publisher, the authors, and the editors are safe to assume that the advice and information in this book are believed to be true and accurate at the date of publication. Neither the publisher nor the authors or the editors give a warranty, express or implied, with respect to the material contained herein or for any errors or omissions that may have been made. The publisher remains neutral with regard to jurisdictional claims in published maps and institutional affiliations.

Cover Image © By Simon Gakhar

Printed on acid-free paper

This Palgrave Macmillan imprint is published by the registered company Springer International Publishing AG part of Springer Nature.
The registered company address is: Gewerbestrasse 11, 6330 Cham, Switzerland

PREFACE

What is the essence of human nature and how might we increase the human capacity for tolerance, prosocial behavior, and developmental growth? Perhaps more importantly, how might we collectively, as a society, work to reduce the ever-increasing problems of conflict and aggression? These are important questions that have been raised by community members, educators, and parents in an effort to help transform our communities to become more resilient, productive, and healthier places to live. Recently, the topics of ethnic conflict, extremism, and aggression have become important global issues given the increasing problems that have been associated with political, economic, religious, and environmental factors. The nature of human conflict and causal factors that are associated with extreme violence, hate crimes, and terrorism (both domestic and global) have remained perplexing problems given their increasing prevalence despite recent international efforts to address these crimes (Al Ramiah & Hewstone, 2013).

There are several reasons why this manuscript is needed today. Both global and local issues (i.e., immigration issues, Deferred Action for Childhood Arrivals [DACA], sanctuary campuses, human rights issues, and climate change) and political rhetoric have recently contributed to environments that (unfortunately) have resulted in increased conflict and violence at unprecedented rates. Crimes against women and vulnerable groups (i.e., human trafficking), intentional homicide, and assault are also increasing globally despite international efforts to address these problems

(Harrendorf, Heiskanen, & Malby, 2010).[1] Increases in racial conflict exacerbated by perceptions of unfair police practices, acts of genocide and ethnic conflict as well as impending nuclear war with North Korea remain consistent themes in the media today. Because of the increased conflicts that we are witnessing within our own communities and abroad, the need to understand the psychological and ecological mechanisms to help resolve these different forms of conflicts is very much needed. This manuscript addresses not only the role of community growth and development as key factors in understanding and reducing extremism and ethnic violence, but also the *obligation* that communities now have to remain proactive in their efforts in protecting human rights and to reduce violence. Recent research (Ellis & Abdi, 2017) has identified a fundamental and consistent theme among resilient communities that have been instrumental in reducing ethnic conflict and violence: social connection. Throughout this manuscript we will examine the importance in providing community residents opportunities to work collaboratively and share their life experiences as a means of reducing bias that contributes to ethnic conflict and to improve the communication and trust that is consistently evident within a healthy community. This manuscript will also address the role of community development and intergroup contact, and examine how different types of group behaviors, such as interdependency, superordinate goals, and community intervention, can help to reduce conflict and promote understanding. An important scope of this manuscript is to increase our understanding of the unique and inherent need for humans to contribute to and volunteer in their community as a means of understanding the importance of diversity and achieve a sense of belonging and connectedness to their community. Our goal in preparing this manuscript is simply to provide the relevant framework and mechanisms in how communities may help with the transformation of what Ervin Staub (2013) describes as a more "peaceful society" that promotes understanding, resiliency, and an appreciation of diverse values. Suggestions for future research that promote community growth, service work, and stewardship activities are also offered.

Hudson, WI   August John Hoffman
2017

---

[1] https://www.unodc.org/documents/data-and-analysis/Crime-statistics/International_Statistics_on_Crime_and_Justice.pdf

REFERENCES

Al-Ramiah, A., & Hewstone, M. (2013). Intergroup contact as a tool for reducing, resolving and preventing intergroup conflict. *American Psychologist*, *68*(7), 527–542.

Ellis, B. H., & Abdi, S. (2017). Building community resilience to violent extremism through genuine partnerships. *American Psychologist*, *72*(3), 289–330.

Harrendorf, S., Heiskanen, M., & Malby, S. (Eds.). (2010). International statistics on crime and justice. Retrieved, from https://www.unodc.org/documents/data-and-analysis/Crimestatistics/International_Statistics_on_Crime_and_Justice.pdf

Staub, E. (2013). Building a peaceful society: Origins, prevention, and reconciliation after genocide and other group violence. *American Psychologist*, *68*(7), 576–589.

CONTENTS

LIST OF FIGURES

Community Development, Stewardship Activities, and Volunteerism: The Evolution of Human "Connectedness" and Interdependency

"Umunto Ngumuntu Mgabamti"
Zulu phrase as quoted by Desmond Tutu ("A person becomes a person through engagement with others") (Jill D. McLeigh (2015). Creating conditions that promote trust and participation by young people … why it matters. American Journal of Orthopsychiatry, *85(6), S67–S69).*

Human nature is complicated in that it can exist and manifest itself often in antithetical and paradoxical ways. Often a contributing factor that influences how individuals engage and communicate with each other may depend more on their *perceptions* of the motivation and common goals shared by different groups and an awareness of intergroup ideologies that promote justice and fairness as well as bias and prejudice (Al Ramiah & Hewstone, 2013). Different arguments historically have promoted different etiological and motivational factors in explaining both helpful (i.e., prosocial) and antisocial behaviors. For example, altruism (the capacity to help others with no expectation of reciprocity) has recently been described as having an evolutionary genesis, where these behaviors actually were shown to be *adaptive* in promoting reproductive fitness and group resiliency (Buss, 2015). In some situations humans have been shown to exemplify altruistic behaviors and make sacrifices for others if they feel that this behavior may

© The Author(s) 2018
A. J. Hoffman et al., *The Role of Community Development in Reducing Extremism and Ethnic Conflict,*
https://doi.org/10.1007/978-3-319-75699-8_1

be reciprocated in the future (Axelrod & Hamilton, 1981), while in different situations, they remain aggressive and opportunistic regardless of environmental circumstances or consequences (Webster, 2008).

Similarly, individuals can simultaneously engage in reprehensible acts of violence and aggression toward out-group members, yet display seemingly selfless acts of kindness and empathy to strangers who appear distressed (Hauser, Preston, & Stansfield, 2014). Psychology has tremendous capacity in influencing human behavior and (if applied correctly) can help individuals to understand one another despite *perceived* differences and to work cooperatively (i.e., civic engagement and community development projects) with others for mutually beneficial goals (Guillaume, Jagers, & Rivas-Drake, 2015; Hoffman, 2015). Similarly, communities that provide residents with opportunities to build relationships and partnerships can establish stronger community resilience and thus prevent youths from engaging in acts of extremism and destruction (Ellis & Abdi, 2017). Scholars, philosophers, and social science researchers have long attempted to understand the essence of human nature and the mechanisms involved that contribute to the development of prosocial and cooperative behaviors that help build communities and strengthen society. Viewing behaviors as simply "good" or "evil," "positive" or "negative" is not a productive (nor accurate) way to view and understand the etiology of human interaction, as a "winner-take-all" or "zero-sum" mentality often increases antagonism among groups of individuals.

In this manuscript, we begin our description of the human condition by understanding and recognizing that ultimately what may define behavior is complex and an interaction among several components (genetics, social and traditional norms, evolutionary history, community structure, and our current environmental climate or *zeitgeist*) that shapes and rewards different types of behaviors. As a result of this description we need to understand more specifically what types of behaviors, ideologies, and cultures were the most adaptive (i.e., cooperative and prosocial) to survival over the millennia of human evolution.

HUMAN CHOICE OR IS "BIOLOGY OUR DESTINY"?

Charles Darwin (1859) is generally credited by most scholars (along with Herbert Spencer and Alfred Wallace) with presenting the earliest and comprehensive theories in human evolution and adaptive strategies in group or community living. More importantly, Darwin described how genetic variation and environmental adaptation were important (but not sufficient) factors in determining whether or not humans survived in a given region or territory or perished. His famous quote "Biology is our destiny" implies that our physical appearances as defined by our genetic history (i.e., phenotypical characteristics and DNA) were essential features that proved to be critical in determining how well a given species could adapt to the physical demands of a given region and climate. In other words, Darwin argued that (biologically) *what* we are defines actually *who* we are and how our decisions are generally made. Certain irrational behaviors that proved to be highly adaptive to specific groups (i.e., territorial aggression, road rage, etc.) during our evolutionary history still remain with us today despite rules and laws in society that attempt to mitigate these primitive behaviors.

Those species that could adapt to the demands of the environment tended to survive and pass those key characteristics on to future generations, improving the overall reproductive fitness of that group. Groundbreaking views within the disciplines of evolutionary psychology and psychology have addressed the topics of natural selection, reproductive fitness, and aggression in an effort to determine how groups interact and exchange those behaviors that have historically facilitated survival (i.e., cooperative alliances). Additionally, psychologists have attempted to understand (and control) how social and environmental factors influence the psychological mechanisms that contribute to and maintain positive behaviors (i.e., prosocial and cooperative interaction) while simultaneously reducing antisocial behavior and conflict. Regrettably, as global populations and technology have exponentially increased, so have specific types of conflict and group violence (i.e., extremism) based on a variety of religious, economic, cultural, and ethnic factors (Ginges, Atran, Sachdeva, & Medin, 2011). Wars are now fought with cell phone technology, improvised explosive devices, and drones. The rapid growth of technology (i.e., social media) has shaped and influenced how we relate and interact with others as well as how we define our friendships or "BFF" (best friends forever). For many persons, technology, social media, and social networking sites (i.e., SNSs) have served as convenient sources of comfort (i.e., "places of belonging") when individuals experience loneliness or rejection from their peers (Knowles, Haycock, & Shaikh, 2015).

Social Media, Technology, and Illusions of "Connectedness"

Gordon Allport (1954) noted in his classic earlier research that there may be significant positive benefits afforded to populations when opportunities (i.e., "real time") of intergroup contact (i.e., volunteer programs and community service activities) exist among community members who share similar goals. Most important in his research addressing the benefits of intergroup contact was that bias and prejudicial attitudes toward traditional out-group (i.e., "minority") members are reduced and negative stereotypes (especially those addressing groups of individuals) are debunked. Once these myths have been debunked, friendships and more productive partnerships are more likely to develop and improve overall communication among diverse groups of individuals. Communities and organizations that provide "real-time" engagement activities and interaction with diverse groups allow groups to see the "real person" behind the negative stereotypes and subsequently reduce the likelihood of conflict based on these negative perceptions (Staub, 2013).

In order for individuals within groups to work most effectively without prejudice, Allport argued that the perceptions (and status) of group members need to remain relatively equal among each other, frequent contact and interaction with each other is needed, and institutional support must exist. Allport further argued that providing individuals with opportunities of real-time (i.e., face-to-face) contact can help debunk common myths and stereotypes that are commonly associated with marginalized groups, thereby providing an environment that encourages mutual understanding and cooperation among diverse groups. This common link that facilitates mutual understanding among different groups is essential in the successful completion of a variety of tasks involving superordinate goals. Providing individuals with opportunities to meet and interact on various types of projects helps to build stronger relationships within groups, which in turn help to reduce prejudice and stigmas that are associated with specific groups. More recently, religious leaders throughout the world have emphasized the value and importance in direct contact with other groups as an effective method to reduce ethnic conflict and violence.

In his address from the Vatican on World Refugee Day (June 20, 2017), Pope Francis urged all people to focus more on the needs of those individuals who are vulnerable, suffering, and fleeing persecution (i.e., refugees). According to recent estimates, over 40 million people have been removed or displaced, with over 2.8 million persons seeking asylum.[1] Pope Francis continued his discussion by encouraging all persons to visit those victims of violence and persecution to help debunk negative stereotypes of refugees. One of the best ways to truly understand people beyond bias and stigma is through direct contact with them: "Personally meeting with refugees dis-

---

[1] *Catholic Herald*, June 27, 2017.

pels fears and distorted ideologies … and becomes a way for people to grow in their humanity as they learn to make room for an attitude of openness and the building of bridges" (Glatz, 2016). Direct contact with marginalized groups and individuals who have been persecuted provides us with a unique opportunity to see them as individuals and dispel myths and negative stereotypes that commonly are associated with victims of oppression.

While some research has identified fundamentalist religious beliefs to be associated with ethnocentric ideology (Banyasz, Tokar, & Kaut, 2016), it is important to note that *individual personality traits* (i.e., social dominance and right-wing authoritarian characteristics) that may have been associated with a particular religion were key variables in determining the existence of ethnocentrism and violent extremist behaviors. Recent research has determined that the benefits afforded to individuals who have had contact and various forms of interaction with victims of oppression (i.e., political refugees) may be generalized to broader populations of individuals (i.e., ethnic minority groups, transgender populations) suffering from similar types of crimes and oppression associated with politically and economically unstable countries (i.e., war crimes, ethnic cleansing, and genocide) (Brown & Hewstone, 2005).

Community Development and "Facebook Depression"

Webster's defines the term "community" as "[a] unified body of individuals typically sharing common interests."[2] The term is actually derived from the Latin concept of *communitas*, which is interpreted as "things held in common." Perhaps one of the beginning points in building a stronger community is in recognizing some of the fundamental values that we do have in common. Humans have an evolved intrinsic need to form close relationships with each other that is vital to both our physical and psychological states of well-being (Dunkel Schetter, 2017). The greater the frequencies of contact individuals have, the more likely they are able to communicate with each other, share ideas, and develop longer and more meaningful friendships (Davies, Tropp, Aron, Pettigrew, & Wright, 2011). In other words, frequent contact with otherwise unknown individuals helps us to discover that we actually have more things in common with individuals we previously did not know. Sharing vital resources with underserved groups can also help create a stronger and more unified community via increased group identity and shared connectedness. If

[2] https://www.merriam-webster.com/dictionary/community.

communities were structured in a way that actually *promoted* volunteerism with frequent cooperative intergroup contact by providing residents with more opportunities for community development and improvement, the likelihood for positive interaction (i.e., trusted friendships) would increase, and prejudice and violence would be significantly reduced (Brown, Vivian, & Hewstone, 1999; Ridge & Montoya, 2013).

The rapid growth of technology within communities has also contributed to how groups engage with and interact with each other as well as how we actually define the construct of "friendship." Increased technologies and social media have provided us with the capacity to communicate and interact with each other without actually being physically present within the group itself, thereby providing a false sense of cohesiveness, which may contribute to a phenomenon known as "Facebook depression" (Blease, 2015). The more time individuals spent on Facebook or similar social media sites that tended to preclude them from engaging or interacting with others directly, the greater the likelihood of experiencing depression or depression-like symptoms. In a recent Forbes study, researchers found that the more people relied on social media to compensate for negative (i.e., depressive) symptoms, the more likely they were to compare themselves with others, which contributed to a wide range of negative feelings, such as low self-esteem and depression.[3] While there may be several reasons why people experience depression (i.e., biochemical and organic factors), the fact that people are now using social media with more frequency and that this has been correlated with depression identifies the importance of real-time interpersonal engagement and how communities may provide opportunities for us to better connect with each other. Communities that sponsor programs that help people work together within a collaborative process (i.e., community "cleanup" days, community gardening programs) have been shown to facilitate a greater sense of belonging, pride, and "connectedness" to their community (Hoffman, 2014). Perhaps one way to help reduce technologically related depression caused by SNSs and social media may simply be a matter of monitoring the (i.e., limited) time spent on electronic devices and participating in more "real-time" events that provide opportunities of engagement and interaction with people.

Humans have evolved for hundreds of thousands of years within environments that provided ample opportunities for multiple forms of interaction—some positive (i.e., cooperation) and others negative (i.e.,

---

[3] https://www.forbes.com/sites/alicegwalton/2015/04/08/new-study-links-facebook-to-depression-but-now-we-actually-understand-why/#1aeb339c1e6d.

antisocial behaviors and conflict). Recent research (Lo Coco, Di Fratello, Giordano, Gullo, & Kivlighan, 2016) has identified the unique qualities groups may possess during actual or "real-time" structured activities in resolving conflicts (i.e., interpersonal problems). Groups that have been equipped with opportunities to engage with each other as equal partners in problem-solving situations have also been shown to be more adaptive and resilient when facing similar types of problems in the future (Kivlighan & Kivlighan, 2013).

In their classic research addressing the dynamics of intergroup contact and how prejudice and ethnic conflict may be reduced, Al Ramiah and Miles Hewstone (2013) have identified modernized alternative forms of virtual contact that have proven to be instrumental in reducing conflict and prejudice: virtual and parasocial contact, extended contact and "imagined" contact (p. 534). "Parasocial contact" has been described as really how media portrays specific groups in desirable or less threatening ways. Media that portrays groups in positive ways (i.e., cooperative relationships and friendships) has been shown to significantly reduce prejudice and conflict. Al Ramiah and Hewstone found that through the mechanisms of parasocial contact and virtual exposure, long-standing prejudice and animosity among Jewish and Arab students in Israel was significantly reduced as well as improved out-group attitudes and perceptions among ethnically diverse groups. Similarly, simply *knowing* that contact is increasing among in-group and out-group members tends to have an ameliorative effect on historically and diametrically opposed groups, a term that is referred to as "extended contact" (Turner, Hewstone, Voci, & Vonofakou, 2008).

THE "ROBBER'S CAVE EXPERIMENT": PROMOTING FRIENDSHIPS THROUGH INTERDEPENDENT GOALS

Gordon Allport (1954) was not the only social scientist during this time studying the impact of group dynamics, contact theory, and reduced prejudice. Muzafer Sherif and colleagues (1961) introduced the concept of realistic conflict theory and illustrated how the structure of environments can shape and influence behaviors in a variety of ways. Sherif's research examined how groups can effectively work together most efficiently and identified the dynamic impact of perceptions of superordinate goals, stereotypes, and competition among groups of individuals. The "Robber's Cave Experiment" conducted by Muzafer Sherif and colleagues (1961) clearly identified the mechanisms in which the environment, community, and group identity influence how individuals perceive and interact with each other, either positively (i.e., through the establishment of cooperative alliances) or negatively (i.e., where competition for resources may influence antisocial behaviors). In this study, Sherif intentionally created highly competitive situations that involved groups of boys at a summer camp located at a state park in Oklahoma as a means of illustrating the dynamic effects of realistic conflict theory and how the development of superordinate goals may help to reduce the conflict that is typically associated with highly competitive environments.

Stage I: In-Group Versus Out-Group Development or the "We–They" Dichotomy

In the initial phase of the experiment (development of the "in-group"), Sherif contrived various situations that promoted a strong sense of out-group animosity and a highly competitive environment among the group ($n = 22$) of boys. For example, both teams (*The Rattlers* and *The Eagles*) wore emblems on their shirts that identified them with their team mates, and each group had their own flag, representing their loyalty to their team. The greater the visual salience of the differences and the distinctions between the two groups of boys, the greater the degree of competitiveness and rivalry evolved between each group. Various competitive games were organized (i.e., baseball, tug-of-war) in a zero-sum (i.e., "winner-take-all") environment that promoted antagonism toward each group. The antagonism was exacerbated when one team was awarded a trophy as a symbolic representation of their superiority over the other group.

Stage II: Competition and Friction

As the groups of boys became more competitive (and openly hostile) toward each other, name calling, taunting, and cabin sabotage became more prevalent. The hostility and competitiveness was also exacerbated by the presence of symbolic representations of each group, including flags, distinct T-shirts representing the colors of the teams *Eagles* and *Rattlers*, and badges. The hostility was also exacerbated by the perception of a zero-sum situation held by the participants. In other words, each group thought that only one group would be awarded the desired goals (i.e., access to water, movies, or food) and this perception influenced antagonism and justification of aggression to the opposing group. Once the hostility and divisiveness among the two groups of boys was achieved, Sherif then created a series of situations (superordinate goals) that required both groups of boys to work together so that each member of each team could benefit.

THE VALUE OF SUPERORDINATE GOALS: DRINKING WATER TOGETHER

Stage III: Integration and Unification

The first superordinate goal addressed a most vital and basic need to human existence: potable water at the camp. The boys in both groups needed to work together to tote water back to their cabins, latrines, and kitchen until the water pump could be repaired. In another superordinate goal, the boys from both groups wanted to watch a movie but the Camp Director did not have enough money to purchase the movie. The boys were then asked to contribute some of their money so that the movie could be purchased, which would allow all of them to see their favorite movie (*Treasure Island*). The reunification and integration of both groups of boys became apparent when they all agreed to dine together as one group during the final day of the summer camp. Sherif's research identifies the salience and importance of how limited resources can quickly impact how we view different groups and how conflict, prejudice, and discrimination develop within groups. Most social scientists agree that the most effective way in which prejudice and conflict arising from limited resources may be reduced is through the establishment of superordinate goals that allow individuals to work productively and collaboratively with each other. A shared environment that teaches cooperative behavior can also remind us that we are more likely to achieve our goals when we work together and communicate with each other—in other words, the true essence of community.

How are the findings of the classic research conducted by Sherif (1961) and colleagues relevant to our society today? Clearly, when individuals perceive others within their community as a viable resource through increased intergroup contact in achieving important materials and resources, we are significantly more likely to create friendships and develop cooperative relationships that can ultimately build stronger and more resilient communities (Davies et al. 2011). Interestingly, specific *forms* or *types* of community service projects that provide opportunities for increased intergroup contact also provide inherent benefits to community members among specific age groups. Structured and organized community programs and volunteer activities for youths (i.e., sport activity programs or environmental education programs) have been shown to increase general positive physical and psychological development, such as enhanced intrinsic motivation and improved concentration levels among youths (Larson, 2000).

Similarly, organized community service activities, schools (i.e., "enviroschools"), and volunteer programs that emphasize ecological and environmental stewardship practices have resulted in adolescents' increased subjective stages of well-being as well as behaviors that improve the ecological and sustainable qualities of physical and "green" environments (Kerret, Orkibi, & Ronen, 2014). Community service and volunteer programs that are designed to help with educating individuals about issues relative to maintaining a "greener" environment have also been show to increase commitment to future environmental programs and increased pro-environmental attitudes (McDougal, Greenspan, & Handy, 2011).

Older adult populations are significantly increasing in the United States given advances in health, nutrition, and medicine. According to recent estimates projected by the 2008 US Bureau of the Census, by 2050, approximately 25% of the population of the United States will be aged 65 or older, and currently one out of every eight Americans is aged 65 or older. Given the significantly increasing role of active older Americans, the role of leisure, volunteer, and service work is important in establishing positive mental health and improved psychological states of well-being. The role and benefits of community volunteerism and service work among designated populations (i.e., older adults) is well documented (Anderson and colleagues, 2014; Bond, 1982). For example, older adults who have participated in community service and volunteer activities have shown to have overall improved cognitive functioning, reduced dementia risk, and improved physical and biological functioning (Anderson and colleagues, 2014). Additionally, seniors who participated in regular and consistent volunteer programs showed significantly less likelihood to develop memory problems, such as impairment (Carlson and colleagues, 2012), and improved subjective mood states, such as increased self-esteem (Fratiglioni, Wang, Ericsson, Maytan, & Winblad, 2000). In general, there is extensive evidence that individuals benefit in many ways when a community is willing to provide a broad range of service and volunteer activities for diverse group (i.e., ethnically diverse groups, older adults, children, etc.) participation.

Community service programs and stewardship activities can facilitate an increased sense of belonging and connectedness to one's community by providing mechanisms for people to work collectively with each other and adapt to accepted norms within the community itself (Fisher & Ackerman, 1998). Increased intergroup contact provided through the development of different forms of community service activities and volunteer programs has established greater means of communication among otherwise polarized and separated groups, which often lead to conflict. The contact hypothesis demonstrates this through multiple and various forms of community service activities. As we have seen, positive intergroup attitudes among community participants and residents can be achieved when various service work and stewardship programs are made available for individuals to participate in.

A greater sense of connectedness within communities is achieved when multiple forms of stewardship activities are provided as opportunities of engagement and interaction among community residents. During this process a common in-group identity is achieved, where individuals no longer view themselves as different from one another but rather as a cohesive and unified group. A good example of this is when a community is recovering from some type of a disaster (natural or human-related), where individuals form cohesive units to facilitate their survival and subsequently build a strong and more unified bond together, such as sharing vital resources (i.e., food and water) and using each other as a support base. Additionally, the added benefits of community service activities and stewardships help to provide a more productive and cohesive link between residents because of a greater sense of common needs, reduced stereotypes, and greater empathy with each other. Community service programs and stewardship activities provide unique benefits to individuals because they facilitate frequent contact with other individuals, with whom normally we would have minimal (if any) contact. Existing research has shown that frequent contact (and less polarization) with diverse groups of individuals can help reduce negative stereotypes and prejudice because individuals are more likely to discover that they have common interests with each other (Brown & Hewstone, 2005).

Additionally, community service activities and stewardship programs provide the framework where frequent intergroup contact has been shown to evolve from animosity (out-group status) to trust and cohesion, which is commonly associated within an in-group identity, originally described by Pettigrew (1998):

Stage 1: The first step involves contact and interaction with different groups of individuals that share a common goal within the community—this may include individuals from different socioeconomic groups, religious backgrounds, sexual identity, and so on.

↓

Stage 2:   The second step involves recognition of mutually important and shared goals. Stage 2 also involves increased communication, discussion, and continued contact with diverse group members. Here, preexisting bias and prejudice may come into question (and gradually debunked) as partnerships are formed within the group.

↓

Stage 3:   The third step involves previous out-group members that are now categorized as in-group members and trust is developed within the group. The combination of increased contact, communication, and work toward mutually beneficial (i.e., superordinate) goals helps reduce bias and prejudice. The "they" in group development have now become "we," which significantly reduces the likelihood of future conflict among groups residing within communities.

Community Service Programs and the "Jigsaw" Approach

Perhaps one of the reasons why community service activities and volunteer programs are so popular among individuals is that they provide a unique environment that enables people from all backgrounds to work together and to share their skills in the creation of a better living environment that is shared by all people. In more successful community service and volunteer programs, people *want* to share their ideas to the group because they feel respected and valued through equal member status and in their capacity to contribute to the group. Community service activities and volunteer programs that are structured in a way that allows *all* members of a group (i.e., students within a classroom, employees in a work environment, or neighbors within a community) to contribute and share their skills are most effective because they help them discover a stronger sense of purpose, community identity, and belongingness.

In many ways, this approach has been compared to a "jigsaw" approach, where members of a group (typically students within a classroom or learning environment) bring forth specific skills that are necessary to complete the community project. Similar to constructing a jigsaw puzzle, each member of the group is seen as distinct and necessary, and "fits" within the group to help complete the project.

Elliot Aronson and colleagues (1978) originally devised the jigsaw approach as a highly successful (and popular) educational tool in primary and secondary grades as a way of engaging all students to contributed shared work on an academic assignment. The value and benefit of the jigsaw approach are numerous in that this methodology may be implemented in many different types of environments (i.e., employment areas, academic disciplines, civic engagement programs, etc.) that allow a broad range of individuals to contribute and share their skills toward a superordinate goal. The jigsaw approach is also unique in that it provides opportunities of learning and education among students (and community members) where all individuals need to cooperate and work cohesively for the best results. The mechanics and operational procedures of the jigsaw approach are also very similar to the basic principles of community service activities and volunteer programs. For example, both procedures encourage (and in some cases require) all members to participate in the completion of the goal, whether it is creating a community garden or a fruit tree orchard, repairing a school, or simply picking up litter or restoring a recreational area, such as a park. For example, an English composition assignment of four students may require a composition on the Industrial Era of the United States. Some students may focus on products that were manufactured, some may contribute by examining the political governance system that promoted manufacturing during this time, and some may examine how trade systems were established and rates of unemployment during their period.

The key points to note regarding the effectiveness of the jigsaw approach is that the methodology embodies the primary characteristics of *intergroup cooperation* as described by Allport's (1954) classic theory addressing group interaction and reduction in bias, prejudice, and conflict. All members within the community service projects are equal in that they are capable of contributing their skills to help reach goals shared by all community members. Additionally, an underlying essential theme of successful community service projects is that *cooperation* and a mutually important and shared (i.e., superordinate) goal is not only optimal but necessary in order for each project to be completed.

Evolution of Group Dynamics

One of the earliest studies to document the evolution and formation of group development was Bruce Tuckman's (1965) classic research on the five stages of group development. In the first stage ("**forming**"), individuals typically meet and discuss the challenges of the goal or project that they are planning to embark upon. According to Tuckman, in this first stage, individuals are quite civil and friendly to one another as introductions are being made. The overall purpose of this first stage is to discuss the nature of the project, methodology, and how to begin. "**Storming**" is the second phase of group development, and it is here when confrontations and challenges develop in terms of roles, decision-making procedures, and disputes. This conflict is a very normal sequence of group development, and an important consideration during this challenging stage of group development is in helping individuals focus on their shared goals and work through conflicts in a collaborative process. The third stage of group development or the "**norming**" stage is characterized by a resolution of conflicts in previous stages and a compromise in terms of how to best achieve goals within a democratic process. This stage is also characterized through tolerance in recognizing individual differences but visualizing that a shared goal benefits all members. In the fourth stage of group development ("**performance**"), individuals now work cohesively in achieving their goal through shared information and recognition that all members have vital information that should be used as a resource in goal attainment.

Sometime later, Tuckman and Jensen (1977) added a fifth and final stage, which they refer to as "**adjourning**" (this final section of group development has also been referred to as "mourning"). This final stage was added to facilitate closure of the group as well as recognition that the goals achieved by the group translated into a successful process. More recent research by Penner (2004) has addressed the dynamic functions of volunteerism in four basic underlying motives for behavior: volunteerism as a form of planned action, volunteer behaviors occurring within some type of organizational dynamic, volunteer behaviors that occur on a longitudinal or long-term basis, and the fact that individuals who are actually engaged in volunteer work are doing so volitionally and not in a coerced or obligatory manner. Similarly, research conducted by Chacon, Vecina, and Davila (2007) has identified that long-term volunteer behaviors are best predicted by the *behavioral intention* of the individual. In other words, the best results in volunteer work occur when individuals clearly articulate their motivation and goals in anticipation of participating in volunteer work. Additionally, Chacon, Vecina, and Davila argue that a secondary contributing factor to successful long-term volunteerism (not surprisingly) is the inherent satisfaction among individuals who are actually participating in their work. Volunteerism that is rewarding, satisfactory, and capable of seeing positive outcomes most likely will enhance the longitude (and future participation) of volunteer work and community service participation.

GROUP DEVELOPMENT AND COMMUNITY SERVICE WORK ACTIVITIES

Similar to Bruce Tuckman's (1965) classic research addressing how groups evolve from several distinct stages, community service activities can also reflect a similar sequence of change and contextual transformation. The initial stage of development in community service work (CSW) activities is characterized by insight and recognition that some form of change is needed within the community itself. Community members may see their neighborhoods deteriorating and wish to work together in an effort to address the problem. Often a group of individuals recognize that in order to improve and develop their neighborhood, they need to work together and cohesively to effect some form of positive change. For example, groups of neighbors may be frustrated with the litter strewn about in their local parks and want to enact change. They may form their own group (similar to the popular "neighborhood watch" programs) and assign cleanup crews to their local parks and recreation areas as well as create a "neighborhood watch" team that reports vandals littering to their local law enforcement agency. The group of concerned citizens has evolved from a disorganized group of individuals to a cohesive unit of individuals achieving goals that benefit both residents and the community itself.

The cycle of community service activities and work (CCSAW) is offered next, which describes the sequence of the stages of community development (see Fig. 1.1).

Stage 1: Community Deterioration

Groups develop among individuals typically out of a shared concern or need that impacts all members who happen to share a particular space or area. The key element to successful participation in different types of CSW activities and volunteer programs can be summarized in one word: opportunity. Providing multiple forms or types of opportunities for CSW activities encourages people from all lifestyles with different sets of skills and trades to work together in the development of a healthier and more resilient community. When we review the differences between holistic and vibrant communities as opposed to neglected and deteriorating communi-

Fig. 1.1 The cycle of community service activities and work (CCSAW)

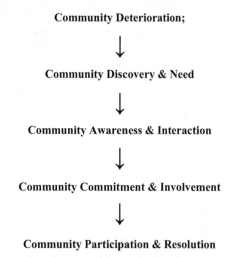

Community Deterioration;

↓

Community Discovery & Need

↓

Community Awareness & Interaction

↓

Community Commitment & Involvement

↓

Community Participation & Resolution

ties, we see that residents within vibrant communities actually *want* to participate and volunteer to build a stronger neighborhood. The drive to build a stronger community has its roots in how residents feel connected to their neighborhoods, combined with a sense of belonging. Additionally, vibrant communities and neighborhoods provide multiple venues that allow individuals to share their skills and participate in numerous ways. A neglected and blighted community is one where the residents do *not* feel connected to their neighborhood and or feel detached or alienated from others living in the area. Community deterioration, neglect, and apathy are also a function of a *lack* of connectedness and belongingness to the neighborhood, typically because of a lack of opportunity to establish goals that will benefit the public. Gangs often develop within deteriorated neighborhoods as a means of identification with a neighborhood that has deteriorated through apathy and neglect. Members of gangs often use symbols (i.e., graffiti) as a means of identifying themselves and territories within the community. Additionally, neglect comes from a perception of apathy or futility where residents feel that they cannot address or correct the problems that they see occurring within their neighborhoods.

Recently (October 2014), a group of students from Metropolitan State University, Inver Hills Community College, and the University of Michigan Dearborn participated in a community development project to help rebuild a neighborhood in Detroit, MI. The neighborhoods of the Detroit community were devastated from the 2008 economic recession, but recently, the city has made advances in the rebuilding of local neighborhoods, largely from individuals becoming aware of the problem and participating in community development programs, such as a community garden. The community rebuilding effort in Detroit started as a result of initiatives from several concerned neighbors and local schools to rebuild the community.

Stage 2: Community Discovery and Need

Community discovery and need refers to the *process* whereby residents of a community have discovered a need to help rebuild their communities into a more healthy, vibrant, and resilient neighborhood. Discovery of the blight and neglect within the surrounding area does not happen overnight, but rather usually through the collective efforts of a few concerned citizens. While much research has been published addressing the effects and impact among intergroup behaviors among volunteers, an essential component in understanding group volunteerism lies in the motivational factors addressing such behaviors. Classic research by Fisher and Ackerman (1998) has identified the importance of reinforcing principles and norms that regulate volunteer and prosocial behaviors. Communities that emphasize the importance of volunteer activities and community service programs through norms and obligation of responsible citizenship have resulted in higher rates of engagement and volunteer behaviors among residents. Similarly, media that reinforces these behaviors through the actions of positive role models engaged in a variety of different types of community service programs may vicariously influence other individuals to engage in similar types of prosocial behaviors (Bandura, 1977; Happ, Melzer, & Steffgen, 2015).

Once the community need of volunteerism and prosocial behaviors have been identified, the incentives and rewards for recruiting volunteers may be demonstrated through the use of media that portrays positive role models engaging in similar behaviors in a variety of community-related improvement projects. Famous actors, athletes, celebrities, and even former presidents can play an important role in recruiting individuals to participate in several different types of community service programs. For example, former President Jimmy Carter is known for his prosocial behavior and community activism in helping to create and build homes for the homeless, and ex-President Obama is also known for his volunteer efforts, which have influenced countless individuals in building stronger communities.

Stage 3: Community Awareness, Interaction, and "Inattentional Blindness": We Do Not Notice What We Are Not Looking For

In order for community development to begin, volunteers, neighbors, and concerned citizens must first actually notice and be aware that a problem actually exists. While it may sound relatively obvious that a dilapidated neighborhood, littered street, or polluted lake needs intervention, change cannot occur until people actually notice that the problem exists and are willing to intervene and correct the problem. Think for a moment about your own personal experiences involving your awareness of the physical structure or surroundings of your own community. How often have you discovered a retail shop, store, or pharmacy that you passed by countless times but never actually noticed until you needed something from one of these stores? According to researchers Dan Simons and Chris Chabris (1999), humans may frequently be exposed to a variety of visually vibrant stimuli within their own communities, but we often are immune to any form of change pertaining to those stimuli, as they occur over time, a term that they refer to as "inattentional blindness." Recent research has shown that when participants are not actually expecting to see events, they become "blind" to things that may be occurring directly in front of them, and this may include the gradual deterioration of a community or neighborhood where we work or reside.

PERCEPTUAL BLINDNESS, GORILLAS PLAYING BASKETBALL, AND COMMUNITY DETERIORATION

Daniel Simons and Chris Chabris (1999) conducted a very interesting study that explains why often people are not aware of important things occurring right in front of them—whether they may be at work, driving a car, or simply chatting with friends over lunch. They labeled the phenomena as perceptual or "inattentional blindness," and the term refers to a type of selective attention where we are essentially blind to a series of unexpected events that may be unfolding right in front of us. In what is now a very famous video that depicts inattentional blindness in a humorous way, subjects were presented with a divided visual attention task where they are asked to count how many times members from one team (each wearing white T-shirts) are throwing a basketball to other team members. The participants watched this video for 30 seconds, and at the end of the video they were not asked how many times the basketball was thrown, but simply whether or not they saw the gorilla in the video. Out of 192 participants, 90% reported not seeing the gorilla walk through the group of individuals throwing the basketball to each other. Think about this for a moment—almost half of the subjects participating in the experiment did not see the gorilla walking through a group of people playing basketball because they were more focused on counting the passes from one team to another.

Previous researchers (Graham & Burke, 2011; Mack & Rock, 1998; Neisser & Becklen, 1975) have replicated these data, confirming the internal reliability of the study. Individuals are surprisingly quite unaware of unexpected events even if these events are occurring directly in front of them within their own neighborhoods. How do the findings of Simons and Chabris (1999) relate to community deterioration and blight? If we become accustomed to events over time, we fail to notice important changes that can impact the overall quality of living among residents within our own neighborhoods. Buildings may deteriorate, public facilities and schools may no longer offer services to the public, the overall quality of living may decline and for many residents, they may not even be aware of these changes until it is too late to intervene.

What tends to happen to several communities over time (especially those communities impacted by economic recession) is the gradual deterioration of the physical and environmental properties that contribute to the aesthetic appeal and beauty of the surrounding area. However, the surprising characteristic is that for many communities, the gradual deterioration goes unnoticed until the problems are so serious that intervention is costly and very time-consuming. Once a community has discovered a need for the implementation of community service and volunteer programs, it is essential for individuals within the community to organize and work together most efficiently.

TAKE NOTICE! TIPS ON KICK-STARTING THE COMMUNITY SERVICE ACTIVITY

1. **Take the initiative and introduce yourself**. People need to know both **who you are** and how the community service project can help them. Once we have become aware of the issues that need changing within our communities, we need to become more directly engaged

with the people who make up the community. Talk to other people living in the surrounding area and get their opinion on how to make positive change more likely to occur. Food is always a great way to meet other people and learn more about the history of your neighborhood. Consider hosting a dinner, luncheon, or barbeque and inviting people to get more input within the community.

2. **Go to the people**. Contact different community members within a variety of different locations. Community centers, school districts, churches, and town hall meetings are all excellent beginning points for you to meet people who make up the community and get feedback on how to make important changes. Also, when people are asked how to help, they are more likely to get involved and provide assistance to you.

3. **Be willing to L-I-S-T-E-N**. When requesting feedback and information on how to make positive change within your community, listen to the people who have been living there. Understanding the issues of the community means that we also need to understand the needs of the people that make up the community. What are the strengths and limitations that make up the community that people live in? What changes would they like to see? When people see that you are willing to help and to listen to their needs, they will be significantly more likely to help you with these goals.

Stage 4: Community Commitment and Involvement: Intrinsic Motivation

Once members of the community have discovered the issues and problems that exist, and the problems of "inattentional blindness," apathy, and neglect have been addressed, the real work within the community may begin. The question remains how to organize community members in such a way that each person may be committed to resolve the problem and the group may work most efficiently. People generally want to become involved in projects where there is support and direction is given to them, especially when they realize that others share their concerns. As a coordinator of community service projects, it is important to remember that all persons have skills and aptitudes that may be applied cohesively with other members to facilitate a successful community project. Getting the word out and publicizing that an important community service project is about to begin is essential for success. One of the most effective and efficient uses of public information is still direct communication (i.e., "word of mouth") to each community member. Going to public forums, food banks, local charities, and service organizations and announcing a brief description of your project can also be very helpful in recruiting individuals for your project. Using social media and online fundraising organizations (i.e., GoFundMe, Razoo, Fundly, CrowdFunding, etc.) and technology can also be very useful for individuals in getting the word out about the project. In some situations, if individuals are not available to assist in the development of your community service activity, then donations may also be available. Once your communication system has been established, make sure that your instructions to the group are very simple and clear. Posting the date and time of the project, as well as getting an idea as to how many people will be involved, is also very important. Make the instructions very consistent, simple, and straightforward. Also, make sure that people have a direct way to get in touch with you if they have any questions.

CSW Activities Should Be Intrinsically Rewarding

People tend to remain committed to a particular project, regardless of whether it is volunteer work or community service related, if they are getting some form of intrinsic reward from it. Similarly, people tend to abandon projects that do not provide some form of meaning, reward, or satisfaction to them. The volunteer project or community service activity must be both meaningful and personally rewarding to individuals if they are going to be committed to a successful activity, especially long-term projects. If individuals are not contributing to the project in a meaningful way or if they cannot see how their efforts are being utilized in the overall development of the project, interest will subside and a higher attrition rate will develop. In other words, people will simply lose interest in what they are doing.

A great example would be local green spaces, urban forestry programs, and community gardens. People will be significantly more likely to continue their volunteer work if they see exactly how their efforts have contributed to the development (and progress) of the garden itself. This is why it is important for students and community residents to not only participate in the initial phase of a gardening program (i.e., cultivating and planting seeds), but also contribute to the process of harvesting the healthy foods and distributing them to the local food centers that serve the low-income families within the neighborhood. As the community garden gradually begins to take shape and increase in beauty and production of vegetables, more people will want to volunteer their services. The most successful community service projects are those where people actually *want* to contribute to the project because of the intrinsic rewards and satisfaction that they receive in lieu of their participation and because they can see that their efforts are actually making a difference within their community.

Stage 5: Community Participation and Resolution

The final component of the CCSAW theory is the actual participation and resolution phase. It is here where individual participants have a full and complete understanding of their role within the scope of the project and they understand when the project itself has been completed. The resolution phase is both a time of happiness and of sadness for many participants. It is a happy experience in that individual members and participants have contributed in a meaningful way in the completion of a community service project that benefits so many other people, but yet also sad in that the project has been completed and their relationships with others (within the context of community service activities) is nearing an end. For many different types of community service and volunteer projects, the work involved is seasonal and continuous. For example, in the upper Midwest regions, community gardens typically begin in mid-to-late May or early June and continue through October. Community members who have participated in the development of a community garden where foods are donated to local charities may create meaningful relationships with other community members in the development of healthy foods for low-income families and look forward to resuming their volunteer service for the following year.

In conclusion, vibrant communities that provide opportunities for individuals to participate in some way in sharing their skills and talents (i.e., community gardening and healthy foods distribution programs) within a collective process enhance positive growth and psychological states of well-being, which are contributing factors to individual resilience and empowerment. People inherently want to participate in a variety of volunteer programs when they feel that their efforts are recognized, appreciated, and needed (Fisher & Ackerman, 1998). Recognizing those efforts among volunteers will also help to ensure continued success of future community service and stewardship programs that are designed to help meet the growing demands among low-income and underrepresented groups.

REFERENCES

Allport, G. W. (1954). *The nature of prejudice*. Cambridge, MA: Addison-Wesley.
Al-Ramiah, A., & Hewstone, M. (2013). Intergroup contact as a tool for reducing, resolving and preventing intergroup conflict. *American Psychologist, 68*(7), 527–542.
Anderson, N. D., Kroger, E., Dawson, D. R., Binns, M. A., Caspi, E., Damianakis, T., ... Cook, S. L. (2014). The benefits associated with volunteering among seniors: A critical review and recommendations for future research. *Psychological Bulletin, 140*(6), 1505–1533.
Aronson, E., Blaneyh, N., Stephin, C., Sikes, J., & Snapp, M. (1978). *The jigsaw classroom*. Beverly Hills: Sage.

Axelrod, R., & Hamilton, W. D. (1981). The evolution of cooperation. *Science, 211*, 1390–1396.

Bandura, A. (1977). *Social learning theory.* Englewood Cliffs, NJ: Prentice-Hall.

Banyasz, A. M., Tokar, D. M., & Kaut, K. P. (2016). Predicting religious ethnocentrism: Evidence for a partial mediation model. *Psychology of Religion and Spirituality, 8*(1), 25–34.

Blease, C. R. (2015). Too many "Friends," too few "Likes"? Evolutionary psychology and Facebook depression. *Review of General Psychology, 19*(1), 1–13.

Bond, J. B. (1982). Volunteerism and life satisfaction among older adults. *Canadian Counsellor, 16*, 168–172.

Brown, R., & Hewstone, M. (2005). An integrative theory of intergroup contact. *Advances in Experimental and Social Psychology, 37*, 255–343.

Brown, R., Vivian, J., & Hewstone, M. (1999). Changing attitudes through intergroup contact: The effects of group membership salience. *European Journal of Social Psychology, 29*, 741–764.

Buss, D. M. (2015). *Evolutionary psychology: The new science of the mind* (5th ed.). Hardcover: Pearson Publishers.

Carlson, M. C., Parisi, J. M., Xia, J., Rebok, G. W., Bandeen-Roche, K., & Fried, L. P. (2012). Lifestyle activities and memory: Variety may be the spice of life. The Women's Health and Aging Study II. *Journal of the International Neuropsychological Society, 18*, 286–294.

Chacon, F., Vecina, M. L., & Davila, M. C. (2007). The three-stage model of volunteers' duration of service. *Social Behavior and Personality, 35*(5), 627–642.

Darwin, C. (1859). *The origin of species.* London: John Murray.

Davies, K., Tropp, L. R., Aron, A., Pettigrew, T. F., & Wright, S. C. (2011). Cross-group friendships and intergroup attitudes: A meta-analytic review. *Personality and Social Psychology Review, 15*, 332–351.

Dunkel Schetter, C. (2017). Moving research on health and close relationships forward – A challenge and an obligation: Introduction to the special issue. *American Psychologist, 72*(6), 511–516.

Ellis, B. H., & Abdi, S. (2017). Building community resilience to violent extremism through genuine partnerships. *American Psychologist, 72*(3), 289–330.

Fisher, R. J., & Ackerman, D. (1998). The effects of recognition and group nee on volunteerism: A social norm perspective. *Journal of Consumer Research, 25*(3), 262–275.

Fratiglioni, L., Wang, H. X., Ericsson, K., Maytan, M., & Winblad, B. (2000). Influence of social network on occurrence of dementia: A community-based longitudinal study. *Lancet, 355*, 1315–1319.

Ginges, G., Atran, S., Sachdeva, S., & Medin, D. (2011). Psychology of the laboratory: The challenges of violent extremism. *American Psychologist, 66*(6), 507–519.

Glatz, C. (2016). Best way to fight terrorism is to warmly welcome refugees. *The Catholic News Service*. http://cathstan.org/Content/News/Pope-Francis/Article/Best-way-to-fight-terrorism-is-to-warmly-welcome-refugees-pope-says/2/193/7260

Graham, E. R., & Burke, D. M. (2011). Aging increases inattentional blindness to the gorilla in our midst. *Psychology and Aging, 26*(1), 162–166.

Guillaume, C., Jagers, R., & Rivas-Drake, D. (2015). Middle school as a developmental niche for civic engagement. *American Journal of Community Psychology, 56*, 321–331.

Happ, C., Melzer, A., & Steffgen, G. (2015). Like the good or bad guy – Empathy in antisocial and prosocial games. *Psychology of Popular Media Culture, 4*(2), 80–96.

Hauser, D. J., Preston, S. D., & Stansfield, R. B. (2014). Altruism in the wild: When affiliative motives to help positive people overtake empathy motives to help the distressed. *Journal of Experimental Psychology, 143*, 1295–1305.

Hoffman, A. J. (2014). Build a fruit tree orchard and they will come: Creating an eco-identity via community gardening activities. *Community Development Journal, 50*(1), 104–120.

Hoffman, A. J. (2015). Community service work and the virtues of apple trees: Planting seeds of hope in the Newtown Victory Garden. *Global Journal of Community Psychology Practice, 6*(1), 1–12.

Kerret, D., Orkibi, H., & Ronen, T. (2014). Green perspective for a hopeful future: Explaining green school's contribution to environmental subjective well-being. *Review of General Psychology, 18*(2), 82–88.

Kivlighan, D. M., & Kivlighan, D. M. (2013). Group climate research: Where do we go from here? *International Journal of Group Psychotherapy, 63*(3), 419–431.

Knowles, M. L., Haycock, N., & Shaikh, I. (2015). Does Facebook magnify or mitigate threats to belonging? *Social Psychology, 46*(6), 313–324.

Larson, R. (2000). Toward a psychology of positive youth development. *American Psychologist, 55*, 170–183.

Lo Coco, G., Di Fratello, C., Gullo, S., & Kivlighan, D. M. (2016). Group relationships in early and late sessions and improvement in interpersonal problems. *Journal of Counseling Psychology, 63*(4), 419–428.

Mack, A., & Rock, I. (1998). *Inattentional blindness*. Cambridge, MA: MIT Press.

McDougal, L. M., Greenspan, I., & Handy, F. (2011). Generation green: Understanding the motivations and mechanisms influencing young adults' environmental volunteering. *International Journal of Nonprofit and Voluntary Sector Marketing, 16*, 325–341.

Neisser, U., & Becklen, R. (1975). Selective looking: Attending to visually specified events. *Cognitive Psychology, 7*, 480–494.

Penner, L. A. (2004). Volunteerism and social problems: Making things better or worse? *Journal of Social Issues, 60*(3), 645–666.

Pettigrew, T. F. (1998). Intergroup contact theory. *Annual Review of Psychology*, *49*, 65–85.

Ridge, R. D., & Montoya, J. A. (2013). Favorable contact during volunteer service: Reducing prejudice toward Mexicans in the American Southwest. *Journal of Community & Applied Social Psychology, 23*, 466–480.

Sherif, M., Harvey, O. J., White, B. J., Hood, W. R., & Sherif, C. W. (1961). *Intergroup conflict and cooperation: The Robber's Cave Experiment.* Norman: University of Oklahoma Book Exchange.

Simons, D. J., & Chabris, C. F. (1999). Gorillas in our midst: Sustained inattentional blindness for dynamic events. *Perception, 28*, 1059–1074.

Staub, E. (2013). Building a peaceful society: Origins, prevention, and reconciliation after genocide and other group violence. *American Psychologist, 68*(7), 576–589.

Tuckman, B. W. (1965). Developmental sequence in small groups. *Psychological Bulletin, 63*(6), 384–399.

Tuckman, B. W., & Jensen, M. A. (1977). Stages of small group development revisited. *Group & Organizational Studies, 2*(4), 419–427.

Turner, R. N., Hewstone, M., Voci, A., & Vonofakou, C. (2008). A test of the extended intergroup contact hypothesis: The mediating role of perceived ingroup and outgroup norms, intergroup anxiety, and inclusion of the outgroup in the self. *Journal of Personality and Social Psychology, 95*, 843–860.

Webster, G. D. (2008). The kinship, acceptance and rejection model of altruism and aggression (KARMAA): Implication for interpersonal and intergroup aggression. *Group Dynamics: Theory, Research and Practice, 12*(1), 27–38.

CHAPTER 2

The Virtues of Community Development and Stewardship: How Communities Respond to Disasters and Build Resilience

In Chap. 1 we introduced a number of concepts related to the implementation and benefits of community service activities. We also examined the role of community service work (CSW) activities and volunteer projects as an effective process in helping bring together diverse community members, and how intergroup contact and superordinate goals can actually help reduce negative stereotypes and improve the overall quality of relationships among diverse community members. When individuals experience a sense of "connectedness" within their communities, they are more likely to work cooperatively and share mutual benefits with each other, while also experiencing less conflict and trauma during times of stress. Similarly, groups of marginalized and underserved populations (i.e., LGBTQ [lesbian, gay, bisexual, transgender, and queer] populations) have expressed a recognition of "need for action" in the healing process and feelings of "community connectedness" when experiencing trauma that has been directed at them, such as the 2016 Orlando, FL nightclub shooting (Jackson, 2017). Their supportive living environment is shaped and characterized more through communication of mutually shared goals (i.e., a safer and more supportive environment) and responsibility in reaching those goals.

Our goals in this chapter are similar in that we will address the virtues and benefits of CSW activities, but describe them more specifically (i.e., environmentally sustainable and "green" activities) in the development

© The Author(s) 2018
A. J. Hoffman et al., *The Role of Community Development in Reducing Extremism and Ethnic Conflict*,
https://doi.org/10.1007/978-3-319-75699-8_2

and rebuilding of those communities impacted by disaster (natural and human-related disasters, hate crimes, and extremism). We will address how a "Victory Garden" has helped rebuild and develop the community of Newtown, CT through the tragedy of the Sandy Hook Elementary School disaster of 2012, and how an urban forestry program continues to rebuild the New Orleans community after the Hurricane Katrina disaster of 2005. We will also explore how the "Living Memorial" Tree Project helped rebuild New York City after the 9/11 tragedy and describe the amazing story of the "Survivor Tree." The Survivor Tree was discovered during the rescue process of 9/11, and many of the survivors and first responders felt that this tree really represented the spirit of the rescue process. When first discovered after the attacks, the tree had been actually uprooted and had only one living branch. Despite the initial trauma, the tree was able to withstand the rubble, smoke, and fire, and now thrives in front of the 2010 Memorial that honor the memories of the victims and survivors of that attack. Finally, we will explore how communities that are impacted through acts of extremism and hate crimes directed toward marginalized groups (i.e., the 2016 Orlando nightclub shooting) can utilize the inherent skills and strengths among the survivors to help rebuild a more environmentally sustainable, resilient, and tolerant community.

In this chapter we will also introduce a new term that is commonly seen in volunteer and community service programs: stewardship. The term stewardship has an interesting history in that its use can be seen in literature and research in the disciplines of history, theology, civic engagement, economics, and psychology. Taken originally from biblical usage, the term "steward" was used as a "keeper of the house" and trusted servant, someone who took responsibility of the welfare of the inhabitants of a private or public residence. The steward's responsibilities ranged from providing nutritious food to all house members and maintaining the well-being of the family to protecting the valuables within the residence of the home he or she maintained. From the theological interpretation, the concept of "stewardship" implies that humans are essentially caring for the welfare of the physical properties and ecological integrity of the environment and the world that we share. We are responsible in managing resources that will be used by future populations that inhabit the earth. In more modern usage, the term "stewardship" refers to the maintenance and care of a particular area that is frequented by people in the public or private sector.

CSW activities and stewardship are terms used commonly to describe how people may work together and share responsibilities that improve the quality of living for a larger group of inhabitants. The majority of stewardship programs are based on values, ethics, and principles of trust, resilience, and health. We will now explore the role of stewardship principles and community resilience within the context of different types of disasters caused by extremist beliefs and ideology. In the first example we will examine how a community in the Newtown, CT area was able to rebuild itself from one of the most tragic shooting events in US history: Sandy Hook Elementary School. As a final note, we wish to emphasize that our focus and purpose in this chapter is in identifying how communities that are impacted by disaster and trauma utilize a variety of natural elements within the ecosystem (i.e., community gardens, atriums, urban forestry programs, etc.) as a means to help rebuild and heal themselves after the disaster.[1]

COMMUNITY RESILIENCE AND DISASTERS: REBUILDING COMMUNITIES THROUGH SERVICE WORK—SANDY HOOK ELEMENTARY SCHOOL

Disasters can occur through a variety of mechanisms—some through natural phenomena, such as hurricanes and floods, and others by human-related events. On December 14, 2012 in a small town (27, 560 residents) named Newtown (Fairfield County), CT, a 20-year-old man committed one of the worst shooting crimes in the history of the United States. Twenty school-aged children attending the Sandy Hook Elementary School (ages of the victims ranged between six and seven years) and six employees of the school district were shot and killed. The shooter had also attended the Sandy Hook Elementary School as a child, but was removed and subsequently homeschooled by his mother. In October 2006 he was prescribed antidepressant medication (Celexa) and displayed classic obsessive-compulsive disorder (OCD) behaviors (i.e., frequent hand-washing rituals, changing his socks over 20 times a day). He eventually refused taking any medications and his OCD symptoms gradually worsened. At the end of the shooting spree the shooter turned his gun on himself, ending one of the worst massacres in US history. The small rural town of Newtown, CT was in shock and left reeling in the aftermath of one of the worst human-related tragedies in US history. What was once a quite rural town in a classic New England–style neighborhood now was the focus of worldwide attention.

---

[1] The names of the perpetrators of these crimes have been intentionally deleted and will be referred to as the "shooter" or "bomber."

The town of Newtown was inundated with national and global out-pourings of sympathy, cards, toys, media attention, and a variety of community resources. A separate warehouse needed to be constructed to house all of the dolls, toys, and gifts from well-wishers throughout the world, and over 11 million dollars had been donated to the community of Newtown, CT as of March 2014. The school shortly thereafter was demolished and students attended a different educational institution (Chalk Hill School) at a different location. A new school was built in July 2016, with the school flagpole as the only remnant from the original building site of the Sandy Hook Elementary School.

One may wonder how (if ever) a small rural community may rebuild and heal itself from such a tragic event. The answer to this question is yes—as painful as it is to recover from trauma, there are things that groups of individuals and residents of the community may do to help rebuild, recuperate, and heal from trauma. In October 2013 several students from Metropolitan State University and Inver Hills Community College organized a community development project to facilitate the healing process of Newtown. A memorial garden was established under the direction and support of the Newtown community members. Fifty different fruit trees (apple tree cultivars from the University of Minnesota) were purchased, and with the collaborative efforts of the community members and school personnel (Principal Dawn Hochsprung), a memorial garden ("Victory Garden") was established to honor the memories of the victims (see Fig. 2.1).

Much research has empirically documented the positive impact that community service activities and volunteer services can have in community rebuilding (Okvat & Zautra, 2011). More recent research (Tidball, Karasny, Svendsen, Campbell, & Helphand, 2010) has identified specific therapeutic healing qualities of community development programs that involve the use of horticultural and "green" intervention modalities, such as the use of urban forestry programs, community gardening activities, sensory gardens, and access to sustainable ecological systems. While research addressing the physical and psychological benefits of green spaces, community gardens, and urban forestry programs has recently gained in popularity and interest, the actual practice of such activities has been in existence as long as human conflict (i.e., war) has existed.

More recently, Kenneth Helphand (2006) has devoted an entire book (*Defiant Gardens*) to the subject of the healing properties of outdoor environmental projects, specifically used as therapeutic tools among those individuals (i.e., soldiers and civilians) who are confronted with the trauma

Fig. 2.1   The Sandy Hook "Victory Garden" Established October 2014

of war, torture, and violence. *Defiant Gardens* examines the therapeutic role of a diverse range of gardens (i.e., stone gardens, vegetable gardens, ghetto gardens, and even "barbed wire" gardens) as a unique form of resilience and coping under the most horrific and inhumane circumstances of war and conflict. Gardens not only provide a therapeutic escape from the trauma of war and conflict in general, but the proliferation of green and sustainable ecological activities can help promote a sense of purpose, clarity, and meaning in an otherwise chaotic and senseless world where pain and misery seem endless. Gardens provide individuals throughout the world with an environment intended for both psychological and physical healing from conflict and chaos in the "outside" world in which we live. A broad range of gardens (i.e., sensory gardens) have been described generally as "healing," "restorative," "therapeutic," and "spiritual." The Victory Garden established with the support of the Newtown community members provided both a physical and a psychological location where survivors and community members could go to reflect and honor the memories of the victims of the 2012 Sandy Hook Elementary School tragedy. The garden represented the psychological resilience, cohesiveness, and strength that continue to exist within the community. Several of the community members had indicated that they did not want this tragedy to define who they were, but rather wanted to implement the strength within the community itself as the defining feature of Newtown. The focus was not so much in what happened in the past, but the hope and positive encouragement that the community held for their future. The student volunteers from Metropolitan State University and Inver Hills Community College wanted to volunteer in building the Victory Garden by providing a "living gift"— several dozen fruit-bearing trees that would continually nourish and bring life to the community that had experienced so much devastation. Several of the Newtown community residents expressed their deep gratitude and a sense of "solidarity" with the student volunteers who helped establish the Victory Garden.

The Victory Garden was particularly meaningful for the community participants because it brought to the fore the healing properties of nature (i.e., a fruit tree orchard and community garden) that could be shared by all members of the community. Each year the community meets in the "Victory Garden" after the tragic event as a means of honoring the memories of the victims and to celebrate their lives. Exposure to and engagement with nature and ecology has healing effects in several ways, and an entire field of study (*biophilia*) has been devoted to understanding how exposure to nature helps us heal in so many ways. Exposure to natural and green environments facilitates our physical healing process in relation to stress disorders and anxiety and helps with pain management. Additionally, exposure to nature reminds us of our own biological relationship with other living organisms. Exposure to sensory and healing gardens reminds us both of our human potential in what we can accomplish and of our limitations and our own "finiteness" within the natural environment.

Hospitals, trauma centers, and residential treatment facilities for older adults and those recuperating from substance abuse are increasingly utilizing sensory gardens as a means of improving and promoting health (Kuo, 2015). Hospital facilities accommodating natural gardens and access to plants, flowers, and trees in their construction and architectural design are also on the rise. Many individuals have expressed a sense of calming and relaxation after particularly stressful days, and recent (Okvat & Zautra, 2011) research seems to validate these claims. For example, individuals recovering from immune disorders, depression, and post-traumatic stress disorders have found exposure to different types of healing gardens to be particularly therapeutic. Exposure to different types of green ecosystems helps individuals recovering from illness by focusing on the *sensory* healing qualities of the environment (i.e., *breathing* in clean air, *listening* to water channel through a stream or brook, *seeing* the beautiful and vibrant colors of the plants and trees, and actually *feeling* the texture of plants and shrubs). Nature provides these ecologically rich experiences while simultaneously helping us to not focus on (i.e., distract us from) the pain that we may also be experiencing and recovering from. The calming and relaxing impact that gardens universally provide to residents may explain the popularity of community gardens and urban forestry programs among communities that have been adversely affected by disasters and trauma.

Hurricane Katrina and the Healing Effects of Trees

Some of the tragedies that impact and affect communities come suddenly and unpredictably, such as the Sandy Hook Elementary School shooting incident. Few individuals would possibly think that a tragedy of such magnitude could occur in his or her small-town community. While planning and preparation can help reduce the negative impact that these tragedies may have on individuals within the community, there is no accurate way to measure the fear and trauma that residents may experience with natural disasters such as the case of Hurricane Katrina. On August 29, 2005, an extremely powerful (some experts had even warned as "unprecedented") hurricane hit the Gulf Coast of the United States that was classified as a "Category 5" (the strongest classification that exists for Hurricanes). While hurricanes can be predicted with some degree of accuracy, the extreme power and magnitude of Hurricane Katrina essentially caught almost everyone off guard, including the residents as well as local weather experts. On August 25, 2005, the tropical storm had weakened somewhat, but after hitting the warm waters from the Gulf of Mexico, the storm rapidly gained strength and was once again classified as a hurricane. Several local residents had commented prior to the hurricane that they would simply "wait this one out" and had no idea of the devastating powerful impact that Katrina would develop. Unfortunately, for those who had decided to stay and bear the brunt of the storm, it had become too late to leave even if they had wanted to. The hurricane and storm had already breached several levees and therefore made travel by car virtually impossible. Loss of life and property destruction were extensive, beginning from the coast of Florida to Texas.

Natural Disasters, Poverty, and Race

Surviving a natural disaster such as an earthquake, flood, or hurricane in itself is horrific. However, experiencing a natural disaster and surviving only to live amid the rubble and destruction while waiting for help that has been delayed by bureaucratic red tape is even more devastating. Prior to the onset of Hurricane Katrina over one million people were living in poverty in the states of Alabama, Louisiana, and Mississippi and these conditions may have contributed to the lack of mobility for residents to move to a safer area before the hurricane actually hit each state. The fact that a greater number of the victims and survivors of Hurricane Katrina were identified as underrepresented groups (i.e., African American) raised skepticism about how government funds (Federal Emergency Management Agency [FEMA]) were being used.[2] The fact that natural disasters such as Hurricane Katrina impacted primarily minority groups has further exacerbated the tension between racial groups and requires mediation and interaction through community service and development programs.

[2] https://www.cbpp.org/research/essential-facts-about-the-victims-of-hurricane-katrina.

While controversies still exist over the exact number of lives lost due to Hurricane Katrina, recent reports issued by the National Hurricane Center place over 1836 lives lost and over 80% of the city being flooded due to breached levees. Additionally, the number of people who were either displaced or relocated has been estimated to be over one million and the overall cost of the Hurricane was a staggering $105 billion for repairs and redevelopment of the community. Perhaps the most disturbing thing about the impact of Hurricane Katrina is that much of the negative impact of flooding *could have been reduced*. Some reports after the flooding had indicated that the US Army Corps of Engineers had used shorter steel pilings in the construction of the levees, walls, and support systems, and that the failure of these construction sites in preventing flooding was the primary cause of deaths for the majority of victims in New Orleans (United States Congress, 2006). In addition to the trauma of the flooding, levee failure, and loss of lives were the delays in emergency responders reaching the survivors in the neighborhoods that were most affected. One agency, in particular, was criticized (FEMA) for the delays in getting help and resources to areas where they were most needed. The primary issue was in getting the most critical resources needed to individuals who were either stranded inside (and in some cases on top of) their homes. Ultimately, FEMA did provide support services to over 700,000 applicants, such as living quarters, trailers, potable water, and food.

PLANTING TREES IN NEW ORLEANS POST KATRINA: REBUILDING THE COMMUNITY OF THE PEOPLE

The defining feature of a resilient community is not the negative impact of the trauma, but rather the *recovery* process and healing of the traumatic events, such as shootings, floods, earthquakes, and hurricanes. Recovery is defined by the inherent belief systems that the survivors have in rebuilding their own communities and regaining a sense of normalcy post the chaos that they have endured. Despite disorganized (and delayed) rescue attempts and distribution of resources, the community residents began rebuilding their own community within just a couple of years. According to researcher and author Keith Tidball et al. (2010), the Hurricane Katrina community survivors began planting trees within their own neighborhoods to bolster their self-esteem and assert community strength and identity. Neighborhoods took on their own unique identities and responsibilities in the rebuilding process and created individual teams of support. Communities identified with the tree-planting project as a way to overcome the depression, pain, and trauma that they experienced in one of the worst hurricanes ever recorded and to affirm their own sense of resiliency. They also wanted to show the world that Hurricane Katrina could not defeat them (despite the media showing otherwise), nor would the bungling mistakes of the government (i.e., FEMA) keep them oppressed in their recovery efforts. In one interview by Tidball et al. (2010) with a survivor from Hurricane Katrina, the survivor noted:

> I am going to go further back (than Katrina) … we lost something … we had these big majestic Oaks that city planning and everyone else saw fit to uproot. Along with those oaks, we had inherited businesses. So that's the legacy that's lost … These trees (we are planting) might be a reminder of what we lost, so that we don't ever forget it and don't let that happen to us again, as well as kind of light a fire under us to ensure that we won't have to worry about a legacy being lost (due to Katrina). (p. 600)

In order for a community to rebuild itself after devastating disasters, such as floods, hurricanes, and earthquakes, it is essential that the community remain inclusive in providing *opportunities* for all individuals to have some input in the recuperation process. In the case of Hurricane Katrina, the magnitude and scope of the devastation were both expansive and extremely expensive. Notwithstanding these formidable challenges, within three to four years, the community has made great strides in rebuilding itself in the development of community resources, such as housing, transportation, and parks and recreation. Several community agencies, non-profit groups, and non-government organizations worked immediately in the aftermath of the hurricane and over 6000 trees were planted in some of the more devastated regions. Neighborhoods in the New Orleans, LA area developed support groups that focused on distribution of these resources that contributed to the development of planting trees along streets that were known for their agricultural and ecological beauty. Additionally, because the interest in planting trees (i.e., Oak trees, Poplar trees) that were native to the area of New Orleans was so popular among the volunteers, a special group named "Tree Troopers" was formulated with individuals who were specially trained in tree-planting practices.

The "Tree Troopers" group worked collectively with the residents of the New Orleans neighborhood in order to try to capture the memories and beauty of the neighborhood prior to the destruction of Hurricane Katrina. Several of the participants in the tree-planting efforts (i.e., "*Ka − Tree-Na*") commented that their work in planting trees along the sidewalks and neighborhoods helped them develop an appreciation of the positive aspect of nature and they appreciated the "calming effect" that working with green and environmentally sustainable projects had on them. The non-profit volunteer group NOLA (New Orleans Louisiana) has already organized with over 65,000 volunteers and has plans to planted over 100,000 trees in the areas devastated by Katrina. More recently, the Department of Parks and Pathways in 2010 established a $750,000.00 grant to the city of New Orleans in planting and has planted over 4000 trees to help rebuild the community.

The different types of trees that would be planted within the neighborhoods of New Orleans with the grant money include the Gingko, Jasmine Blueberry, Chinese Fringe Tree, Alta Magnolia, and Dahoon Holly tree. Many of the volunteers who participated in the neighborhood tree-planting projects (i.e., Treme neighborhood) worked collaboratively with trained arborists to help rebuild the community that had lost so much because of Katrina. Most importantly is the fact that the actual residents and survivors from the devastating impact of Hurricane Katrina have worked together and empowered themselves in rebuilding their own communities through urban forestry programs. Their successful rebuilding efforts are continuing today and are gradually transforming their communities and neighborhoods to a thriving environment.

The 9/11 Tragedy, the Living Memorials Project, and the "Survivor Tree"

Prior to the 9/11 terrorist attacks the United States was not at war and few people were familiar with the names of terrorist groups that are literally common place today (i.e., Al-Qaeda, ISIS [Islamic State of Iraq and Syria]). Traveling to an airport really did not require much preparation, and thinking about what types of items could be included in a suitcase was an irrelevant topic for most people. After 9/11 however, our world has changed irreversibly, with safety and security measures being updated and implemented in airport security terminals, public sporting events, and so on. The impact of 9/11, as well as the rescue efforts of the "first responders," was unprecedented. After the collapse of the south tower at 9:59 am, the communications systems among the responders, police, and fire personnel became severely limited, which also contributed to the casualties list. Any available support staff helped to prevent further loss of life, and even animals (i.e., over 400 working dogs) were used in the recovery process. Since the devastation on 9/11, over 250 additional support organizations have been established as a means of helping with the rebuilding process and have raised over $700,000 for victims' families.[3] Additionally, the National September 11 Memorial & Museum was established on May 21, 2014, which commemorates the 9/11 attacks. In just over three months after its opening, the museum boasted of hosting over one million people.

The Transportation Security Administration developed shortly after the 9/11 terrorist attacks and, in 2003, was incorporated into the Department of Homeland Security. The events of 9/11 triggered one of the longest wars in US history (Afghanistan) and provided the impetus in the development, in 2002, of the Guantanamo Detention facility, which still operates today, albeit under controversy among civil libertarian groups. Although there are some disagreements regarding the exact number of lives lost during the 9/11 attacks, most reports estimate 2996 lives being lost, with over 6000 injured that day (Morgan, 2009).

Post 9/11: Healing Trees at Ground Zero

Shortly after the tragic terrorist attacks of 9/11, Congress commissioned the US Department of Forestry for the development of the Living Memorials Project, where literally thousands of different types and species

---

[3] https://en.wikipedia.org/wiki/September_11_attacks.

of trees would be planted to honor the memories of the victims. In May 2010 one of the first Oak tree groves to be planted was at Ground Zero at the Memorial Plaza. Here over 400 Oak and Sweetgum trees were planted to preserve and honor the memories of the victims at the World Trade Center. The World Trade Center has been described as a leader in "eco-friendly" and sustainable environments that will accommodate trees each year in an effort to preserve the memories of those killed and injured during the 9/11 attacks.

The fact that some living things (human, plant, or animal) can survive some of the worst tragedies is a wonder in itself. A devastating forest fire can leave hundreds of acres scarred and burned, with seemingly no life remaining, but only after a few months, we begin to see the telltale signs of reemerging life. First a few strands of green grass, then some flowers (i.e., "fireweed" is common), and after a few years, nature has transformed a bleak and desolate area into a thriving green area. This phenomenon was apparent with the now-famous "Survivor Tree" of the 9/11 tragedy.

Sometime during the extended recovery process, rescuers noted an unusual biological event—amidst all of the strewn and twisted metal and debris stood a lone tree. First, there was an uprooted branch extending from the debris, but then the rescuers were able to determine in the extrication process that the tree was still clinging to life. The tree itself had been twisted and gnarled during the original bombing attack of 9/11, but somehow managed to survive in the rubble. The tree was discovered in October 2001 at Ground Zero and was affectionately named the "Survivor Tree." The Survivor Tree is actually a Callery Pear Tree (*Pyrus calleryana*) and, upon its discovery, was carefully uprooted and transplanted in a recovery area monitored by the New York City Department of Parks and Recreation. The discovery and therapeutic recovery of this tree are significant in several ways. The Survivor Tree was capable of surviving despite having only one living branch and being slightly damaged and uprooted during a storm in 2010. Still the Survivor Tree lives, and for many people, it represents the resiliency and spirit of the people who experienced one of the worst attacks on US soil. The tree is available for visitors to see and marvel at how life continues despite trauma and conflict. Similar to the Newtown Victory Garden, where several fruit-bearing trees were planted to honor the memories of the victims of that tragedy, the Survivor Tree of the 9/11 terrorist attacks represents the spirit and fortitude of the survivors and also honors the memories of those 2977 lives lost on that fateful day (Fig. 2.2).

Fig. 2.2   The Survivor Tree (2010): Callery Pear Tree (*Pyrus calleryana*)

THE 2016 ORLANDO NIGHTCLUB SHOOTING

Disasters can strike anywhere in the world and impact a few individuals or tens of thousands of lives. Disasters may be intentional for a variety of reasons (i.e., political or religious ideologies) or occur through acts of nature, such as hurricanes, floods, and earthquakes. The disasters that we have discussed thus far have included a shooter at an elementary school in Newtown, CT, the 9/11 attack of the World Trade Center, and the devastating effects of Hurricane Katrina in the city of New Orleans, LA. Extremist behavior and hate crimes can be directed at groups or individuals based on religious beliefs and political ideologies. In the case of the June 12, 2016 Orlando nightclub shooting, one individual engaged in the most destructive mass shooting in the history of the United States at The Pulse nightclub located in Orlando, FL. During that particular week, The Pulse was hosting "Latin Night," and as a result, the majority of victims were of Hispanic descent. The shooting at The Pulse nightclub was essentially politically motivated, where the shooter had claimed that he wanted the

US interventions in Syria and Iraq to end and to "stop the bombings" of these countries. Additionally, shortly before the attacks, the shooter had called a news agency (News 13 of Orlando) and claimed allegiance to then ISIS leader Abu Bakr al-Baghadadi.

After a three-hour standoff with the Orlando police, the shooter was killed by a SWAT team after negotiations had failed. After the shooting (5:53 am), a total of 49 individuals at The Pulse nightclub had lost their lives, with another 53 individuals wounded in the attack. Several of the victims had either texted or phoned friends and relatives of the attack as it occurred, but many were also confused with the loud music and were not sure what was happening around them. The Orlando nightclub shooting ranks as the deadliest single-shooter incident in US history and the deadliest attack against the LGBTQ community.[4]

2016 MEMORIAL PAVER GARDEN OF ORLANDO, FL

Shortly after the 2016 Orlando nightclub shooting, the community worked rapidly together to facilitate the healing process. The Orlando Memorial Paver Garden was established and opened on September 26, 2016 near the location of the nightclub where the shooting occurred. Each of the 49 victims will have a paver bearing their name to honor the memories of their lives and their contributions to the community. Additionally, a petition has developed with over 1000 names requesting a rainbow-colored crosswalk near the location where the shooting took place. It is hoped that the pavers and rainbow-colored crosswalk will help people to remember this tragic event and how a community can help with the recovery process of disasters.

The community members of the Orlando shooting quickly organized to help with the recovery efforts. In just nine hours, over $767,000 dollars was raised for the families of the victims and also to help with the cost of the rebuilding efforts of the community. Specific corporations within the Orlando community donated significant amounts of money and resources to help with the rebuilding efforts (i.e., The Walt Disney Corp. and NBC Universal each donated over one million dollars). In addition, since the shooting, the City of Orlando has announced that a deal was made to purchase The Pulse for a total of $2.25 million dollars with the intention of developing the area as a memorial to the public. Furthermore, the plans for the memorial include artwork (i.e., screen-wraps) that highlights the lives of the victims.[5]

[4] https://en.wikipedia.org/wiki/2016_Orlando_nightclub_shooting.
[5] http://www.orlandosentinel.com/news/pulse-orlando-nightclub-shooting/os-pulse-nightclub-orlando-update-20161107-story.html.

COMMUNITIES BEGIN THE HEALING PROCESS

In this chapter we have summarized different types of extremist and traumatic events that have impacted several communities, beginning with the Newtown, CT shooting, the Hurricane Katrina disaster, the 9/11 terrorist attacks, and, finally, the Orlando, FL shooting at The Pulse nightclub. All of these tragic events have several common themes that can illustrate how a community may begin the healing process. First, in each tragic event that has impacted a community, regardless of whether it is an extremist event, a natural tragedy such as a flood or an earthquake, or a senseless shooting, the healing process comes from the people themselves *coming together* to share their feelings, their pain, and their hopes for the future. In times of crisis and tragedy, quite simply, people are highly vulnerable and need support from friends, families, and neighbors. It is a time to reflect upon the damage and loss that has occurred, but also a time to begin planning how to recuperate and heal from the tragedy. The survivors of a tragic event first evaluate the damage done to the community, care for their survivors, and share in the responsibility of rebuilding. A second common theme in the recovery process among community development is that the survivors and victims of the tragedy refuse to allow this event to define their lives or the course of development within their own communities. They resolve themselves to pick up the pieces of a broken community and cooperate in the development of a stronger and healthier environment. We saw this cooperative resolve first among the community members of the Sandy Hook Elementary School shooting as they quickly constructed the "Victory Garden," then with the survivors of Hurricane Katrina and 9/11 in the development of urban forestry programs, and, finally, with the survivors of the Orlando shooting in the development of a paver memorial area to honor the memories of the victims.

As we have seen in the earlier classic research by Gordon Allport and Muzfer Sheriff, when tragedy strikes, humans have a psychological predisposition to interact, collaborate, and help others (regardless of religious, ethnic, or economic identity) in rebuilding their own communities. This predisposition has served as the glue that has helped humans survive trauma and conflict over millions of years of evolutionary development and still exists today (Allen-Arave, Gurven, & Hill, 2008). The capacity for human social exchanges helped our species adapt under extremely adverse conditions (i.e., draft, floods, hurricanes) and is manifested through common group behaviors and alliances, such as reciprocal altruism (Trivers, 1971) and the "tit-for-tat" principles commonly seen in the "prisoner's dilemma" (Axelrod, 1984).

As a community begins to heal, we need to focus on the positive components (i.e., skills and traits) that people can provide only when they realize we are strongest when we work together. While much research has developed over the years addressing the psychological impact of trauma and extremism, little research has actually addressed the different types or forms of psychological bonding and connectedness that is common after traumatic events impact a community. Current research by Ellis and Abdi (2017) has identified the specific types of psychological connectedness and bonding among individuals that occurs post violent extremist events:

(A) Connections to those whom we know and are familiar with: the social connections that are referred to as "bonding" (a sense of belonging to those that we perceive as similar to us)

(B) Connections to those whom we perceived as being different from us: "bridging" (a sense of belonging to those whom we perceive as somehow different from us, such as in ethnicity, religion, and social class)

(C) "Linking" (a sense of connection or partnership that is developed through agencies and commerce, such as government offices, business stakeholders, and community buildings)

Ellis and Abdi (2017) have described humans having a central trait or tendency to form relationships and collaborate with each other in spite of perceived differences as a means of overcoming the trauma they have just experienced. This resiliency is not only essential to individual healing, but also a requirement among communities that facilitates empowering individuals in the aftermath of the trauma that they have experienced. Similarly, much research has addressed the common factors that communities possess during times of disaster and trauma. Norris, Stevens, Pfefferbaum, Wyche, and Pfefferbaum (2008) have specifically identified four qualities that are vital for any community to overcome trauma and continue in the development of resilience: economic growth and development, continued information and communication within the community, social capital, and community competence. In this extensive analysis of resilience and how communities may most efficiently respond to disaster, the authors identify no less than 21 different descriptions of resilience and its application in a variety of disasters, ranging from natural events, such as floods and hurricanes, to human-related tragedy. The authors have completed a meta-analysis of resilience theory and have integrated these concepts in a way that describes how communities may respond to disasters and adversity in the most efficient way by utilizing existing community resources.

Social capital is considered to be a vital asset to the concept of resilience because it provides a way for community members to essentially use each other as a viable source of information in the recovery process post disaster. Social capital may be instrumental in identifying the various resources that may be implemented within the recovery process post disaster and can be utilized among neighbors, families, and friends. Social capital is versatile in the sense that close relationships among neighbors and community members may result in more efficient information being disseminated through the community itself and provide critical information to individuals who lack traditional communication systems (i.e., cell phones and the internet). Thus, social capital may be reflected within a variety of mechanisms and across different economic levels. Another important factor that defines resilience and how efficiently a community may rebuild itself post disaster is reflected through economic development and existing resources. Much research has identified that lower-income neighborhoods that are negatively impacted by disasters have a significantly higher rate of psychological distress because of the inequities in distribution of resources (Norris and colleagues, 2002a).

The psychological distress and health-related problems involving lack of resources in the rescue efforts of victims of disasters were most evident in the 2005 Hurricane Katrina disaster, where over 60,000 survivors in New Orleans relied on rescue efforts, which were delayed due to communication problems and bureaucratic problems associated with local and state authorities, including FEMA. As Quarantelli (1994) notes, an increasing problem associated with disasters is the increasing deterioration of infrastructure, such as bridges, tunnels, and roads. In the 2005 Hurricane Katrina disaster, over 80% of the city of New Orleans was flooded and two-thirds of the deaths occurring in that city were due to levee and floodwall destruction caused by faulty construction materials. Given this alarming information, we can see how inequities that are distributed in the construction of infrastructure, combined with fewer resources and mismanagement within government systems, can exacerbate the problems experienced by low-income communities.

INFORMATION COMING IN AND INFORMATION GOING OUT

A third area that contributes to community resilience according to Norris et al. (2008) addresses the role of reliable information and how it may reach different populations of individuals during times of crisis and tragedy. According to the authors, a central or primary contact source (i.e., "hotline" or "911") is essential to people so that they may quickly access critical information. While it may be true with some catastrophic events that prediction is difficult to determine (i.e., earthquakes or human-related tragedies, such as mass shootings), a central and reliable source of information that can be trusted by community members is essential. One other point that Norris and colleagues make that is equally important relative to information is the kind of stories that are told by the survivors, or information going out of the community. The authors note that a collective process whereby survivors are able to share their stories of survival in spite of the trauma going on around them is essential to a community being able to survive and reflect resilience to its inhabitants.

Finally, "community competence" has been described as the capacity for a community to learn how to adapt to current or ongoing adversity and remain proactive in developing problem-solving solutions to avoid reoccurring trauma and catastrophe. Community competence is a concept that is more directive about how communities display their abilities to recover from a variety of challenges, including substance abuse, community violence, and disasters. A community reflects competence and resilience in different ways depending on the nature of the trauma and tragedy it has experienced, but there are some overarching themes, including collective action among residents. Collective action allows groups that have been directly impacted by the tragedy to make decisions for themselves. Collective action can also inspire an important psychological phenomenon known as "self-efficacy" (Bandura, 1977). Whereas an individual's general belief system in what he or she can do given a variety of tasks is more relative to self-esteem, Bandura argues that individual perceptions of coping behaviors are based the types of experiences and consequences one faces in times of stress and conflict. Belief systems are shaped by the success of our ability in facing obstacles that are typically found in either mundane tasks or community tragedies, where we rely on the collective efforts of our neighbors to survive.

Finally, the concept of community competence is described where individuals develop an empowering belief system where achieving life-sustaining goals is dependent on the support, cooperation, and collaborative efforts of *all* individuals. Current research (Sturmer, Benbow, Siem, Barth, Bodansky, & Lotz-Schmitt, 2013) has shown an interesting correlation between altruistic and prosocial traits and a significantly more positive attitude toward diverse populations and foreigners (i.e., *xenophilia*). Communities that provide greater opportunities for these kinds of service work and stewardship programs are then more likely to help individuals communicate and understand one another, which will result in reduced ethnic conflict based on negative ethnic stereotypes. The magnitude of the effects of community competence and resilience is determined by the collective actions and recuperative efforts of those community members who have been impacted by a particular crisis and utilizes the skills of individual members to facilitate the recovery process. This belief system defines the true essence of what "community" actually means and reflects the trust that emerges among groups of individuals during times of crisis and stress.

REFERENCES

Allen-Arave, W., Gurven, M., & Hill, K. (2008). Reciprocal altruism, rather than kin selection, maintains nepotistic food transfers on an Ache reservation. *Evolution and Human Behavior, 29*, 305–318.

Axelrod, R. (1984). *The evolution of cooperation.* New York: Basic Books.

Bandura, A. (1977). *Social learning theory.* Englewood Cliffs, NJ: Prentice-Hall.

Ellis, B. H., & Abdi, S. (2017). Building community resilience to violent extremism through genuine partnerships. *American Psychologist, 72*(3), 289–300.

Helphand, K. (2006). *Defiant gardens: Making gardens in wartime.* San Antonio, TX: Trinity University Press.

Jackson, S. D. (2017). "Connection is the antidote": Psychological distress, emotional processing and virtual community building among LGBTQ students after the Orlando shooting. *Psychology of Sexual Orientation and Gender Diversity, 4*(2), 160–168.

Kuo, M. (2015). How might contact with nature promote human health? Promising mechanisms and a possible central pathway. *Frontiers in Psychology, 6*, 1093.

Morgan, M. J. (2009). *The impact of 9/11 on politics and war: The day that changed everything.* Basingstoke: Palgrave Macmillan.

Norris, F. H., Friedman, M. J., Watson, P. J., Byrne, C. M., Diaz, E., & Kaniasty, K. (2002a). 60,000 disaster victims speak: Part 1. An empirical review of the empirical literature, 1981–2001. *Psychiatry, 65*, 207–239.

Norris, F. H., Stevens, S. P., Pfefferbaum, B., Wyche, K. F., & Pfefferbaum, R. L. (2008). Community resilience as a metaphor, theory, set of capabilities, and strategy for disaster readiness. *American Journal of Community Psychology, 41*, 127–150.

Okvat, H. A., & Zautra, A. J. (2011). Community gardening: A parsimonious path to individual, community, and environmental resilience. *American Journal of Community Psychology, 47*, 374–387.

Quarantelli, E. (1994). *Future disaster trends and policy implications for developing countries*. Newark, DE: Disaster Research Center.

Sturmer, S., Benfow, A. E. F., Siem, B., Barth, M., Bodansky, A. N., & Lotz-Schmitt, K. (2013). Psychological foundations of xenophilia: The role of major personality traits in predicting favorable attitudes toward cross-cultural contact and exploration. *Journal of Personality and Social Psychology, 105*(5), 832–851.

Tidball, K. G., Krasny, M. E., Svendsen, E., Campbell, L., & Helphand, K. (2010). Stewardship, learning, and memory in disaster resilience. *Environmental Education Research, 16*(5–6), 591–609.

Trivers, R. L. (1971). The evolution of reciprocal altruism. *Quarterly Review of Biology, 46*, 35–57.

United States Congress. (2006). *A failure of initiative: Final report of the select bipartisan committee to investigate the preparation for and response to Hurricane Katrina*. https://www.loc.gov/item/2006360984/

The Evolutionary History of Aggression and Ethnic Conflict: Why Polarization Fuels Hate and Violence

Conflict has existed as long as humans have existed and is exacerbated by the fact that in many different situations and environments, people have needed to share limited resources vital for their survival. Conflict has recently been described as "the problem of the century" and, unfortunately, has proliferated among both urban and rural areas as societies become increasingly polarized (Fiske, 2002). Hate crimes, ethnic violence, extremism, and increasing aggression (both direct and indirect) seem to impact our society on a daily basis, especially through media outlets and social networking sites. According to the most recent available Federal Bureau of Investigation statistics, violent crime (i.e., assaults) has increased 4.1% in 2016 and homicides have increased 8.6% in the United States.[1] There are many complex reasons why ethnic violence and extremism have existed for centuries and why these problems have become so pervasive within our society.

As a leading researcher in social science, Ervin Staub (2013) has argued that extreme violence and genocide can be somewhat predicted through a combination of cultural, economic, social, and psychological factors that often merge when few community intervention practices are available. Violence, extremism, and hate crimes develop in a multitude of ways and can have long-term devastating effects on the healthy development of individuals

---

[1] http://www.washingtontimes.com/news/2017/sep/25/violent-crime-homicides-us-rise-fbi/.

© The Author(s) 2018
A. J. Hoffman et al., *The Role of Community Development in Reducing Extremism and Ethnic Conflict*,
https://doi.org/10.1007/978-3-319-75699-8_3

as well as destroy the fabric of viable community growth and development. Despite recent evidence that has described the numerous psychological benefits of social interdependence among isolated and ostracized groups of individuals (Uskul & Over, 2017), younger populations of individuals are rapidly becoming radicalized in different cultures that have become increasingly polarized and are at risk in becoming both perpetrators and victims of community violence (Hardaway, Sterret-Hong, Larkby, & Cornelius, 2016).

The fact that many leading researchers have identified the problems of aggression and violence as a complex but predictable set of variables should be reassuring in that communities may develop a variety of intervention programs to help address the problem. Knowing what types of conditions may trigger violent and aggressive behavior may help communities identify intervening strategies to help reduce the onset and frequency of these kinds of problems.

For example, those cultures that emphasize the important role of attentive parenting (Newton, Laible, Carlo, Steele, & McGinley, 2014) and teaching self-regulatory principles that embrace fortitude, moral courage, and "active bystandership" (Staub, 2005) to younger populations will help prevent future ethnic conflict and related problems (i.e., bullying) from developing and increase children's prosocial behavior (Flook, Goldberg, Pinger, & Davidson, 2015). Children are more likely to develop key social skills such as fortitude and "stand up" to support their peers who have been victimized by bullying when they have been provided with basic skills and instruction by schools and their parents. Conversely, a lack of exposure and isolation from ethnically and culturally diverse programs, combined with authoritarian parenting styles, can also directly contribute to ethnocentric ideology and conflict (Negy, Shreve, Jensen, & Uddin, 2003; Smith & Myron-Wilson, 1998) associated with antisocial behaviors. Today, perhaps more than ever, the global community needs to identify the cultural and psychological mechanisms that transform ethnic conflict into understanding, tolerance, and cooperation. In short, as educators and community stakeholders, we need to build a more communicative, interdependent, and, ultimately, more tolerant society.

Getting to Know One Another: Collaborative Community Service Activities

Recent research has identified numerous social, psychological, and physical benefits to communities that provide opportunities for participation in different types of volunteer and community-oriented programs (i.e., urban forestry), civic engagement, and community service activities (Putnam,

2000; Al-Ramiah & Hewstone, 2013; Walter, 2013). Those communities that improve the overall quality of living by providing greater access to key resources (i.e., schools, health-care systems, and nutrition) will have lower rates of crime and aggression within neighborhoods. Recent research has also identified key factors (i.e., economic recession, styles of parenting, etc.) as being significantly correlated with an increased risk of child-related behavioral problems and antisocial behaviors, such as vandalism, substance abuse, and aggression (Schneider, Waldfogel, & Brooks-Gunn, 2015). Additionally, community psychologists have determined that when children have been provided with instruction on how to resolve conflict via improved communication and negotiation with their peers, the rates of conflict are significantly reduced (Goldstein, 1986).

Prevention-oriented community development programs that incorporate practices and skills that are specific to indigenous cultures (i.e., music, art, and growing healthy foods from refugee's native land) have also been shown to be highly effective tools in helping new immigrants adapt to their new community and can also reduce stigma (Nazzal, Forghany, Geevarughese, Mahmoodi, & Wong, 2014). A society that utilizes preventative mechanisms and understands how to implement these mechanisms (i.e., development of interdependent goals and community service work activities) will help bridge cultural divides and strengthen itself by recognizing the multitude of skills and aptitudes that diverse groups inherently possess and need to share within a community environment (Weine, 2011). Similarly, communities that endorse polyculturalistic ideologies and provide opportunities for community members to engage with and communicate directly with religious and ethnically diverse groups showed significantly more openness and positive attitudes to different cultural groups and Muslim Americans (Rosenthal, Levy, Katser, & Bazile, 2015). Stated more simply, when communities provide opportunities with diverse groups to learn about different cultural, ethnic, and religious practices, they are more likely to feel less threatened and understand one another without conflict.

Given the history of ethnic conflict and violence, it is important to evaluate how groups of individuals living within communities may utilize specific methods to help reduce these problems in a more proactive and communicative process. We will now review three of the more common theories as to why aggression and ethnic conflict have evolved and continue to be problematic within societies. We will also explore some of the contributing factors that have recently exacerbated acts of violence toward specific immigrant and ethnic groups: frustration–aggression theory, media and observational learning, and biological–evolutionary factors.

FRUSTRATION–AGGRESSION THEORY OF AGGRESSION: VITAL RESOURCES AND ECONOMIC FACTORS

When is the last time you felt as though you really needed (or deserved) something critical to your overall state of well-being (i.e., getting a good grade in class or earning a promotion at work) and you did not receive this award? Perhaps a coworker was awarded with the promotion that you felt you deserved, and if you are like the vast majority of people, you probably were very upset and frustrated. If we feel as though we deserve something and are denied that opportunity, we typically react with anger and are more likely to become involved in conflict. The frustration–aggression theory (Dollard, Miller, Doob, Mowrer, & Sears, 1939) has argued that a natural and biologically reasonable reaction to not securing vital resources is anger. In a series of studies and empirical research showing what happens to individuals when their goals have become blocked, the degree and likelihood of subsequent anger and violence significantly increase (Green, 1998). During economic recessions, for example, ethnic violence and hate crimes directed toward minority-group members significantly increase (Green, Glaser, & Rich, 1998), as they (underserved groups) tend to become targets of blame for undesirable economic recession by dominant-group members. Classic research by Hovland and Sears (1940) showed an alarming negative correlation between lynchings among African Americans and the price of cotton in the South. As the price of cotton tended to drop during the Great Depression, the number of assaults and lynchings significantly increased. During this period of economic hardship, local farmers and community members who relied on the income provided by the sale of cotton became increasingly disappointed with the rapid decline of cotton. According to the Hovland and Sears (1940) classic study, the farmers and community members had *displaced* their anger and frustration to minority populations due to their increased lack of income and debt (Green et al., 1998).

The findings of the Hovland and Sears (1940) study and more recent studies addressing the adverse effects of economic recession and hate crimes provide important information if we wish to address the increasing problems associated with ethnic hate crimes and extremism. When individuals are no longer capable of maintaining a quality of life that they have been accustomed to due to economic factors, frustration develops and, ultimately, a target is selected as the cause of these negative changes. For example, it may be a common psychological phenomenon for dominant-group members within a community to identify recent ethnic groups as the cause of a variety of social and economic problems, such as economic recession (Velasco & Dockterman, 2010), or simply discriminate against an under-represented group because of their perceived religious identification (Awad, 2010). Several other factors, including rates of arousal (Zillman, 1971) and even atmospheric temperatures, have been attributed to increases in conflict and aggression in athletic events. More recent research has identified a somewhat less robust relationship between economic factors (i.e., "macro-economic downturns") and crimes directed toward protected groups, such as same-sex couples (Green et al., 1998). Practices such as increasing the minimum wage to a more reasonable (i.e., "living wage") level can help better serve underrepresented groups who are trying to provide essential resources to their family members and significantly reduce the likelihood of conflict associated with the availability of these resources.

MEDIA AND OBSERVATIONAL LEARNING: REWARDING VIOLENT BEHAVIORS

While there is clear evidence addressing the relationship between increased frustration and aggression, more recent research has identified learning and observational theories as central factors that are associated with the problems of increased violence. The media today essentially teach younger populations that violence is instrumentally a highly effective method in dealing with a variety of threatening situations, and that positive role models frequently resort to using violence in achieving their goals (Bushman & Huesmann, 2013; Bandura, 1977). Additionally, younger populations understand basic principles of conflict management through their educa-tion with their parents and through observations of perceived positive role models in the media. Particular strategies used by positive (i.e., physically attractive) role models in resolving conflicts are most likely emulated by the viewer, and this process occurs during "real-time" activities as well as through vicarious means.

How children form relationships and bond with parents has also recently been identified as a key factor in conflict management. For exam-ple, those children who may have formed poor relationships with their parents (i.e., avoidant relationships) are more prone to experience vio-lence in their own personal relationships with other adults (Bank & Barraston, 2001).

Other areas of research have identified predisposing factors and situational variables as leading contributors to the problem of violence directed toward other groups in society (Huesmann & Kirwil, 2007). In more recent research the problems of the media associated with gratuitous violence are so pervasive that even dream content while sleeping has been impacted, suggesting that our thoughts can be influenced through the media while we are both awake and asleep (Van den Buick, Cetin, Terzi, & Bushman, 2016).

Exposure to violent media (i.e., video games) and social entertainment systems has become a controversial topic of study given the rapid proliferation of electronic devices that are made available to the public and specifically younger populations. According to Huesmann (2010), a leading factor in the explanation as to why aggressive and violent media content has been linked to violent behaviors, especially among younger populations, is that it portrays violence as essentially a justifiable method of responding to a variety of situations that may exploit others and provoke a combination of negative emotions. Huesmann (2010) also notes that the risks of exposure to antisocial and violent media are strongly linked to increases in aggressive behaviors (especially among male adolescents), and those individuals who disagree with this overwhelmingly strong evidence (i.e., Ferguson & Kilburn, 2009) are more likely to cite "methodological flaws" of the research report as the contributing factors to increased violent behaviors. Unfortunately, a cycle of violence emerges that combines economic factors with the classic theories of frustration–aggression theory and observational learning theory. A "perfect storm" of violence is created where shortages of vital resources (i.e., employment, health care, and educational opportunities) gradually increase with a growing population of individuals who are struggling to provide the minimum essential food, housing, and health care for their families.

As communities struggle with fewer resources and members of underrepresented groups face increasing economic hardships, the likelihood for them to actually become targets of violence, hate crimes, and extremism is increasing significantly. Research has also shown that children who are exposed to violence and aggression in the household (i.e., intimate partner violence) have an increased risk in experiencing a variety of psychological, social, and emotional problems (McDonald, Jouriles, Ramisetty-Mikler, Caetano, & Green, 2006). Immigrant groups rapidly become the scapegoats of violence and extremist activities when resources become scarce. Issues related to ethnic conflict have become exacerbated by media outlets that portray "Alt Right" marchers and White nationalists claiming that the economic problems such as unemployment and recession are primarily the result of increased immigration populations.

VIOLENCE IN CHARLOTTESVILLE, VA

On August 11 and 12, 2017 a group of White nationalists participated in a rally that portrayed a vast array of anti-immigrant slogans, Nazi Confederate flags, and White supremacist ideologies. These far-right protesters were soon confronted by counter-protestors who claimed that their city of Charlottesville, VA was "not a place for racism and xenophobic hate crimes." Tragically, a car allegedly driven by James Fields (a White nationalist sympathizer) plowed into the crowd, killing one woman and injuring 19 of the counter-protestors. The rally was prompted by the discussion of community members to remove the traditional Robert E. Lee statue that was located in Emancipation Park, along with other Confederate memorabilia that was located in the park. Governor Terry McAuliffe declared the situation a "state of emergency," and the Southern Poverty Law Center declared this tragedy as a hate crime. The members of both groups became highly agitated and fought for what they believed was their right to protest, which was protected under the 1st Amendment. The counter-protestors argued that they would not tolerate any hate crimes in their community and chanted: "No hate … no fear … immigrants are welcome here."[2]

Unfortunately, the message of communication, solidarity, and dialogue to preserve peace was overshadowed by media outlets explicitly identifying the aggression, violence, and mayhem as the appropriate response to a tense situation. Younger viewers witnessing these events either by traditional media outlets (i.e., television) or live streaming perceive violence as the appropriate method and process to achieve goals, suggesting more of a "the ends justify the means" mentality among viewers.

BIOLOGICAL–EVOLUTIONARY FACTORS

The interesting characteristic involving aggression is that it seems to be gender specific in determining its frequency and how (i.e., under what circumstances) it is manifested (i.e., direct physical violence). Violence and aggression related to jealousy are problems that are universally problematic,

[2] http://www.latimes.com/local/lanow/la-me-protests-charlottesville-20170813-story.html.

involving men (Archer, 2004) and the drive to secure potential mates as a means of increasing reproductive fitness (Ainsworth & Maner, 2012). An additional factor that contributes to gender differences in displayed aggression is differences in parental investment among offspring and intrasexual competition among other males competing for ovulating females. If patterns of aggressive behaviors and violence were primarily a learned phenomenon in different cultures, we would expect to see at least some variability where females showed greater propensity toward direct violence. However, this is *not* the case. In virtually all cultures and geographic regions within the world, males are the leading causes of violence and aggression, especially within the context of acquiring access to potential females showing greater reproductive value (i.e., genetic fitness) for their offspring (Archer, 2013). Given this unique and consistent cross-cultural paradigm involving male-related violence and reproductive fitness, an evolutionary and biological analysis of how both men and women have evolved patterns of behaviors (both cooperative and antisocial) is timely and requires further exploration into what Parker (2006) refers to as the "conflict between the evolutionary interests of the two sexes."

Aggression has existed literally for thousands of years because it simply works in helping people acquire vital resources, reproductive fitness, and procreation, as well as wards off potential future threats to resources necessary for survival. In short, aggressive and violent behaviors are at least *temporarily* successful. Recent empirical evidence has identified numerous benefits of aggression in how groups survive and describe the psychological effects of aggression as an "evolved solution" to common problems involving the distribution and consumption of food, territory, and potential mates for reproductive purposes (Buss & Shackleford, 1997). While there are undoubtedly numerous negative consequences to highly aggressive actions, from an evolutionary perspective, aggression has become quite utilitarian in the advancement and survivability of our species. For example, Buss and Shackleford (1997) have identified several long-term benefits that aggression has provided among small group communities: gaining access to vital resources, such as food, water, and land. Whether it is a superpower nation that invades a smaller country for its rich crude oil or military assets or a nine-year child bullying other children for candy at a school playground, aggression remains a highly instrumental tactic in acquiring a variety of resources.

Another advantage to the proactive use of aggression is in preventing future attacks by potential rivals and threats. In his 1983 Strategic Defense Initiative, President Ronald Reagan delivered his now-famous "Peace through Strength" and "Weakness Invites Aggression" speech as an essential initiative in maintaining a dominant yet peaceful relationship with other countries with developing military arsenals. The "Peace through Strength" initiative argued that a country that presents the most advanced defense systems available (i.e., nuclear arsenals) can help deter potential future threats from other countries who may consider a preemptive attack.

Evolutionary psychologist David Buss cites other numerous adaptive long-term benefits through the use of aggression, such as reproductive fitness (the use of intimidation and threats of aggression can help males gain access to more fertile women and increase one's reproductive capacity) and "paternity certainty" (the use of aggressive tactics keeps other males from poaching your mate). The term "homicide adaptation theory" has been offered by Buss (2005) to help explain under what circumstances are people (i.e., typically males) most likely to become violent and exhibit highly aggressive (i.e., murderous) tactics. Male sexual jealousy has been noted as a leading contributor to domestic violence and battery against a spouse. Under certain types of situations involving threats and competition for vital resources, males specifically have utilized specific traits (i.e., evolved instrumental aggression) to acquire and secure these resources. Key situational factors, such as spousal fidelity, vital resources (i.e., food, water, land, or crude oil), and threats of war from other countries that have displayed threats (i.e., intercontinental ballistic missile testing) have historically been the key flash points that have triggered wide-scale conflicts. However, an evolutionary predisposition for some individuals to behave aggressively under specific conditions does not mean that this is inevitable or has to happen. Indeed, knowing what types of factors are most likely to trigger conflict and aggression is the best tool in countering and reducing these actual behaviors from manifesting.

Five Factors Associated with Extreme Violence

Social scientist Ervin Staub (2013) has described violence as a phenomenon that exists when several factors merge together (i.e., economic, sociopolitical, and interpersonal), which can help explain the violence that we are currently witnessing in our communities on an increasing level (i.e., Charlottesville, Virginia). Often, these factors may begin as minor escalations and (without some form of intervention) develop progressively into larger conflicts: life struggles and difficult living conditions, cultural characteristics, previous (unhealed) exposure to trauma, passive bystander effects, and inherent personality traits and qualities (see Fig. 3.1).

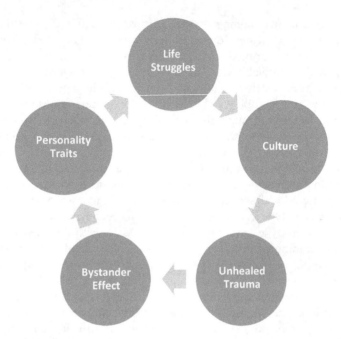

Fig. 3.1 Five factors associated with the origins of extreme group violence (Staub, 2013)

LIFE STRUGGLES AND ECONOMIC HARDSHIPS

Staub (2013) argues that group violence and conflict are most likely to develop within communities that ignore the need for humanistic development and do not provide opportunities for individuals to collectively contribute to community growth. Difficult living conditions, such as economic insecurity (i.e., unemployment), and deteriorating health conditions can initially lead to group polarization and scapegoating; however, poverty itself has not been found to be a primary contributing factor to aggression and violence (Hardaway, Larkby, & Cornelius, 2014). Other factors, including styles of parenting, bonding, and authoritarian communication styles (i.e., low communication with little explanation of rules) with offspring, have been linked to aggression and violent behaviors among specific populations, such as male adolescents (Paschall & Hubbard, 1998). Observable physical characteristics and other phenotypical traits that are associated among immigrant groups and persons of color have been strongly associated with group violence (Hamby, 2015; Hennessy-Fisk 2015; Abu-Ras & Suarez, 2009; Goldsmith, 2014) as well as belief systems that challenge traditional conservative and dominant-group practices (Ruiz, Gallardo, & Delgado-Romero, 2013).

Recent immigrant groups, unfortunately, have rapidly become the scapegoats for many socioeconomic problems that currently exist in communities. Additionally, immigrants may have recently been perceived as "burdens" on economic development and are typically considered "security risks" that typically get singled out in lines at airports and terminals (Green et al., 1998). Current data suggests that although legal immigration rates continue to increase, the flow of undocumented or unauthorized immigration has significantly been reduced, especially since election of President Trump (Velasco & Dockterman, 2010). Similarly, a continuing misperception among dominant-group members that contributes to group violence is the negative stereotype of immigrants as being uneducated, poor, and a primary drain on resources, such as education, trauma, and health care (Ruiz et al., 2013). When discussing the rates of health among new immigrants, it is interesting to note that a substantial portion have been recognized as physically healthy, with actually a lower rate of heart disease when compared with other natural-born citizens living in the United States (Portes & Rumbaut, 2006; Ruiz, Steffen, & Smith, 2013). In addition to maintaining ideal physical health standards, many recent immigrants from collectivistic cultures report psychological needs such as feeling closer to and connected with the community in which they reside (Hoffman, 2014). The psychological forces that typically bring individuals together (i.e., reports of community connectedness) within residential neighborhoods and communities may also play a role in identifying cultural differences among newer immigrant groups (Piff, Martinez, Stancato, Kraus, & Keltner, 2012).

Recently, there has been an increase in identifying the mechanisms that help develop communities in becoming positive and desirable places to live. Community development programs typically incorporate features within close proximity that allow individuals to share time with each other and interact during their leisure. Al-Ramiah and Hewstone (2013) have identified three important elements to successful community development programs: active participation, intergroup contact among community members, and psychological interdependency in achieving specific goals. Additional research has shown that specific traits among individuals (i.e., altruistic and prosocial attitudes) can influence individuals to make more pro-environmental behaviors to improve their neighborhoods and ecological landscape (i.e., using more public transportation) (Pelletier, Lavergne, & Sharpe, 2008). Psychological interdependency refers to a reciprocal relationship requiring cooperation among all group members to achieve a mutually beneficial goal. Neighborhoods and communities that provide community service work and civic engagement opportunities (i.e., community gardening and urban forestry programs) can actually serve as ideal environments that help bring people from different ethnic groups, nationalities, and economic classes together and improve inter-ethnic communication and reduce violence (Shan & Walter, 2015). Community service activities and civic engagement projects help community members from different ethnic and cultural backgrounds discover similarities shared by one another while working toward mutually beneficial goals (i.e., refurbishing schools, creating recreational park systems, and creating community gardens), which can also enhance social capital (Alaimo, Reischl, & Allen, 2010). More specifically, some forms of community service projects (i.e., urban forestry and community gardens) can offer unique opportunities for empowerment from individuals suffering from debilitating psychiatric disorders (i.e., schizophrenia) (Myers, 1998) or help provide meaning in one's life to Jewish prisoners of war, who knew that their chances of survival were very slim due to patterns of genocide and anti-Semitic practices that were common practices among German soldiers during World Wars I and II (Helphand, 2006).

CULTURAL PRACTICES, CONFLICT, AND AGGRESSION

The term "culture" is profound in that it has important influences on the development and growth of individuals, which in turn determine how the values and ethics are invested within a community. In short, understanding the culture in which one lives means essentially being a part of it and participating in a variety of activities that help bring individuals (and groups) closer. Cultures often shape and define the values and processes that contribute to meaningful interaction and provide the mechanisms in sharing and understanding knowledge that helps people to better understand one another. Cultures can also define how we perceive what is "normal," justified, or accepted behavior as opposed to violent or antisocial behavior, and challenging long-held practices that often violate human rights and can result in serious personal consequences, such as arbitrary imprisonment, torture, or even execution (Staerke, Clemence & Doise, 1998).

Merriam-Webster defines culture as "[t]he habits, belief systems and traditions of a particular group of people." Culture has an important influence on the perception of aggression among different groups of individuals. Some cultures may teach individuals that aggression is warranted when reputations and honor have been besmirched (i.e., "cultures of honor"), whereas other cultures view this behavior as inappropriate or immature. Additionally, many standard descriptions and interpretations of aggression often address the *intention* of the act itself.

Aggression is viewed as an intentional, overt, and deliberate act to cause harm to another person. Aggression may be carried out impulsively or deliberately for profit (i.e., "instrumental" aggression). With respect to concepts and practices relative to multiculturalism, the term "culture" refers more to respect and a peaceful coexistence of different belief systems sharing a similar physical location or territory. The concept of culture is becoming increasingly important as our worlds are becoming gradually smaller and contact with others is becoming more common. Many disciplines within psychology and sociology have attempted to understand the psychological mechanics of aggression in an effort to reduce its occurrence. The concept of "global psychology" refers to the practice among community psychologists who are mindful of different behaviors without applying value judgments (i.e., "normal" versus "abnormal" behaviors), which can facilitate a more peaceful coexistence with culturally diverse groups (Berry, 2013).

While aggression and conflict have been recorded in virtually all environments where humans engage and interact with each other, recent research has shown that cultural differences and values have profound influences on the rate, distribution, and types of aggressive actions. For example, many individuals may avoid a direct form of confrontation (i.e., physical conflict) with a rival coworker, but engage in covert or indirect (i.e., spread malicious rumors) conflict. Additionally, the types of cultures that we are exposed to where values and ethics are taught early on in development can have a profound influence on how aggression is justified within that culture (Hofstede, 1980). For example, those Eastern cultures (i.e., China) that emphasize the importance of group work, selfless actions, and volunteerism (i.e., collectivism) have characterized overt aggression as a highly selfish, immature, and egoistic behavior (Forbes, Zhang, Doroszewicz, & Haas, 2009). Conversely, those countries that typically exhibit individualistic attitudes (i.e., United States) typically view aggression as being justified when asserting and defending personal rights and freedom. Recent research has also determined an inverse correlation between the reduction in collectivistic values and increased rates of direct aggression. In other words, as attitudes and values that are directed to helping others within the group or community begin to dissipate, conflict and aggression are more likely to increase within that community. Within individualistic cultures, often a gender effect develops where women are more likely to display indirect aggression to other women (i.e., spreading false rumors), whereas males are significantly more likely to engage in direct conflict and aggression (i.e., physical assaults) with other males (Forbes et al. 2009).

A final contributing factor that has been associated with culture and violence is the *type* of rearing relationship that parents may have with their children. Staub (2013) has identified specific types or forms of parenting (i.e., authoritarian) to be associated with groups of individuals who are actually more accepting and tolerant of tyranny or autocratic ruling styles and less likely to intervene in government practices (i.e., civil disobedience) that interfere with human rights. Additionally, in most Asian cultures, respecting authority, obeying rules and laws, and social conformity are very highly praised and valued practices (Chien, 2016). As a consequence, children and adults who are exposed to authoritarian styles of ruling are less likely to challenge and question authoritarian practices, even in situations where human rights violations are occurring (Milgram, 1974). Authoritarian rulers have also been identified to impact judicial systems and court proceedings that determine guilt or innocence when individuals display civil disobedience and defend human rights, often at the risk of incarceration (Cheesman, 2011). In sum, cultures have historically a profound influence regarding the existence and proliferation of authoritarian rulers and whether or not citizens have tolerated (or objected) to the continued practice of violent and unethical regimes that commit genocide and human rights violations.

Continuous Exposure to Group Trauma: Rebuilding from Ground Zero

Many individuals believe that conflict and violence have become an inevitable by-product of human existence, and that these problems have evolved into systemic public health issues, especially among youth and younger populations (Sood & Berkowitz, 2016). As ethnic conflict and acts of terrorism increase worldwide, negative stereotypes and bias against specific ethnic groups who have been associated with those actions have significantly increased, as have subjective reports of individuals feeling "less safe" and vulnerable within their communities (Abu-Ras & Suarez, 2009). A key problem is false or negative stereotypes that depict ethnic minority groups in a detrimental way despite the numerous contributions that ethnic minority members provide to the community (Carter, 2007). Additionally, false or negative stereotypes contribute to suspicion, hatred, and, unfortunately, extremist actions, which further polarize groups within the predominant society and community.

Prior to the tragic events of 9/11, most Americans took much for granted when engaging in routine aspects of their lives—traveling to the airport, going to a shopping mall, or attending a large public event, such as a concert or sporting event. These events were typically considered normal and mundane, where the most stress experienced may have been waiting in lines or traffic. However, since 9/11, these naïve assumptions have all but disappeared. The 9/11 tragedy consisted of a series of planned and coordinated attacks by the terrorist group Al-Qaeda, and the damage to the World Trade Center and surrounding areas (i.e., Lower Manhattan) was overwhelming. Over 6000 people were injured and 2996 lives were lost, with estimates of over $10 billion dollars' worth of damage to infrastructure in the surrounding area. There were both extensive physical and psychological casualties (i.e., stress, trauma, pain, and suffering), which are impossible to accurately record. Unfortunately, the catastrophic consequences of that horrific event are still unfolding. According to Staub (2013), the *combination* of several traumatic events such as the 9/11 tragedy can directly contribute to escalated violence through ethnic hate crimes, extremism, and aggression.

The negative impact of traumatic events such as terrorism not only contributes to numerous negative physical (i.e., increased blood pressure) and psychological consequences (i.e., stress, chronic depression, posttraumatic stress syndrome, and anxiety), but also has been attributed to increased discrimination and harassment to ethnic and religious groups (Arab and Muslim populations) who have been associated with terrorist groups (Abu-Ras & Suarez, 2009). Additionally, the number of crimes committed against the Muslim population and Arab Americans have increased over an alarming 1700%.[3] The fact that a significant number of crimes involving Muslim Americans and those individuals who appear to

---

[3] American Civil Liberties Union, 2002.

have Middle Eastern traits and characteristics are occurring because of their outward physical appearance is alarming and, unfortunately, contributing to a very dangerous pattern of continued hate within our communities. White nationalist groups are engaging in more violent demonstrations and perpetuate the negative stereotypes and false information that further endangers immigrant families.

The trauma continues unfortunately from the original tragedy that occurred on 9/11 and now through the bias and harassment that occurs from negative stereotypes that are attributed to innocent persons, who only seem to share physical traits with those responsible for the terrorist actions. Although the tragic actions of 9/11 occurred over 16 years ago, almost half (40%) of the Americans interviewed reported some type of bias toward Muslims and 22% indicated that they would not want to have a Muslim as a neighbor (Saad, 2006). Empirical research has also documented that because of the increased negative stereotyping among Muslim populations residing in the United States, a significant number of them (i.e., over 1200) are being detained illegally under clandestine circumstances or deported *en masse* (over 20,800) (Eggen, 2003).

Bystander Effect

Think back to a moment where perhaps you may have actually witnessed a disturbing event or crime. The event could have been obvious and blatant, where you may have witnessed an assault, or it could have been less egregious, where you experienced a "micro aggression" (a flippant or casual insult directed toward any member of a marginalized group) directed perhaps against a colleague or coworker. Did you (or others) try to help, intervene, and assist the victim or did you continue on with your work, not sure perhaps what the appropriate action should have been? In 1968, social psychology researchers Bibb Latane and John Darley conducted very important research addressing the circumstances why certain people may intervene (often risking their own safety) to help others, while others seem to be immune to the needs of others and simply do not become involved in any emergency situations. The classic research conducted by Latane and Darley (1968) is remarkable in that it has one of the highest replication rates in all of empirical science. The researchers were able to predict with reasonable certainty when many individuals intervene and assist in an emergency when several characteristics of a given situation emerge (i.e., the emergency must be perceived as authentic and real, emergency situation requires immediate intervention, etc.). Conversely, as the group census increases, there is a predictable rate of non-intervention by witnesses to the event or crime. Bystander effect refers to the fact that the greater the number of people who are exposed to a particular emergency event, the less likely anyone will intervene and help in the situation.

The important research conducted by Latane and Darley (1968) was actually inspired by a tragic incident in 1964 in Queens, NY involving a woman named Kitty Genovese. Kitty Genovese was walking home alone late one evening and was brutally attacked by an assailant. There were some initial screams and the attacker fled, but when no one called the police, the attacker returned 10 minutes later and murdered her. After police reports were taken the following day, it was determined that 38 witnesses indicated that they heard her screams for help, but each witness thought that someone else had contacted the police. The researchers, Latane and Darley (1968), assumed that the lack of intervention on the part of the 38 witnesses was not due to their callous or insensitive behavior, but rather due to "diffusion of responsibility." The theory of diffusion of responsibility refers to the fact that when a group of individuals witness a crime, each thinks that someone else in the group will report the crime to the authorities and thus fail to intervene. The greater the number of people within the group, the less likely anyone will take responsibility and help the victim.

Overcoming Bystander Effect: Building Stronger Communities Through Group Cohesiveness

Kitty Genovese suffered a tragic death because those witnesses who saw (and heard) the crime gradually unfolding thought that other people would intervene on her behalf. It would be inaccurate (and unfair) to characterize those people who refuse to intervene and help in a situation as "insensitive" or "uncaring." The lack of intervention was primarily due to the concept of diffusion of responsibility—witnesses (incorrectly) assuming that other people are helping the victim. The "Kitty Genovese" tragedy occurred primarily because the community in which she resided (Queens, NY) lacked an important key element in community development: connectedness. Community service activities and development projects provide unique advantages and benefits to residents in that the community rapidly becomes improved through the cohesive actions of the group. When community members feel a strong sense of connectedness and cohesion, they are significantly more likely to experience personal responsibility to intervene and help victims in times of emergency (Rutkowski, Gruder, & Romer, 1983).

The perception of a group as a whole and as a central unit contributes to a greater likelihood of taking on responsibility for individuals who may become victimized among those people feeling directly connected to their community. Thus, one key element (and outcome) of community service work is that it provides and instills a sense of cohesion that promotes a greater sense of personal responsibility to potential victims within the group itself. Communities that provide opportunities for increased contact and interaction among residents will also provide an increased awareness of feelings and emotions among individuals within the group. The capacity to share an understanding of what others may be experiencing and feeling has been referred to as empathy and has been shown to be inversely correlated with aggression (Miller & Eisenberg, 1988). Communities that provide opportunities of interethnic contact and collaboration can thus reduce actions of aggression by increased empathy and personal responsibility to helping others in distress (Abbott & Cameron, 2014) and cyberbullying cases (Machackova & Pfetsch, 2016). A cohesive community can provide residents with a more robust, viable, safer, and more resilient environment through the collective work that is performed by all group members. Recent research (Staub, 2013) has also shown that if we wish to increase the traits of personal fortitude and responsibility that stimulates active bystandership in emergency situations, then we need to provide opportunities for individuals to experience what victims commonly feel during episodes of victimization (i.e., bullying).

More recent research has demonstrated that intergroup contact not only is effective in helping groups resolve conflicts among one another, but can also help reduce tension cause by political conflict and help dominant groups support marginalized groups and pro-minority issues (Ulug & Cohrs, 2017). Intergroup contact and increased awareness of political issues through the use of narratives have also been identified as a key area in helping minority and dominant groups understand one another through shared communication. For example, researchers Ozden Ulug and J. Christopher Cohrs (2017) examined the utilitarian benefits of creating narratives for pro-Kurdish and pro-Turks groups, and found that attitudes toward reconciliation among both groups significantly increased when intergroup contact and narratives were presented to both groups. The researchers found that the narratives helped provide a more personal and humanitarian approach to groups that historically were perceived insensitive or uncaring to them and thus helped facilitate a more conciliatory approach to groups previously considered as "enemies." The results support the theory that a key factor that is necessary in helping to resolve conflicts (even those political conflicts that have existed for centuries, such as the conflict between Kurds and Turks) is possible when a variety of factors (i.e., situational and environmental) can be adjusted to increase contact and interdependency among the groups.

PERSONALITY TRAITS AS INDICATORS OF VIOLENCE AND ALTRUISM

Perhaps one of the most compelling characteristics and attributes of human interaction, dialogue, and engagement is that of human personality. Ask anyone why (or why not) they are attracted to someone and most likely the topic of "personality" will enter into the conversation. Personalities have been described as enduring qualities that describe the whole person, as he or she typically behaves within a variety of different situations. In essence, the personality defines who we "are" as a person and how others may actually view us. The concept of personality is profound in determining how our relationships are formed with other individuals and has been used as a measure to describe individual values, preferences, unique traits, and personal characteristics. The more popular an individual tends to be, the more likely he or she is accepted within intimate social groups. Research has shown that some of the more favorable personality traits (i.e., extroversion) have been associated with a variety of positive characteristics, including increased sociability, communication skills, and a general increase in popularity among peers and colleagues (Ilmarinen, Vainikainen, Verkasalo, & Lonnqvist, 2015).

An individual's personality is considered typically stable and an important asset and tool in determining how social relationships are formed and maintained, and often is used as a measure of one's skills in social interaction. Recent research has explored a broad description of how personality traits may influence individual behaviors in group settings, often ranging from very prosocial and altruistic (Bierhoff & Rohmann, 2004; Carlo, Eisenberg, Troyer, Switzer, & Speer, 1991) to highly aggressive and egoistic (Ainsworth & Maner, 2012; Archer, 2013), and in some cases gender specific (Hanish, Sallquist, DiDonato, Fabes, & Martin, 2012).

An individual's behavior and personality type that has been character-ized as "aggressive" or "violent" may be due to several factors, but leading research has identified aggressive personality types as having an evolution-ary advantage in terms of kin selection, securing resources, and warding off threats and predators (Buss & Duntley, 2008). From an evolutionary perspective, an aggressive personality trait would have presented numer-ous benefits to individuals (i.e., typically males) who were primarily con-cerned with securing resources for kin and smaller clans, increasing reproductive fitness, and mate guarding (Archer, 2013). Not all individu-als (thankfully) share similar aggressive personality traits and characteris-tics. If this were the case humans could not have survived given the numerous environmental threats that existed over the course of evolution. While recent socioevolutionary (Buss, 2015) and biological theories have described aggression as both an adaptive and an evolved trait that played a key role in the distribution of resources and reproductive fitness, other theorists (i.e., Sigmund Freud) have described aggression as a more detri-mental quality that served as an innate function and contributed to the deterioration of cooperative behaviors and social interaction.

More recent research has also shown that while antisocial personality traits have evolved over time as an adaptive mechanism relative to human survival, so too have prosocial and altruistic personality traits, often referred to as the "altruistic personality" (Bierhoff & Rohmann, 2004; Bierhoff, Klein, & Kramp, 1991). An altruistic personality is really more of a combination of several traits that support collective and cooperative means of coexistence. A combination of traits such as the capacity to understand and experience what others may be feeling (i.e., empathy), an inherent belief in a fair and just world (i.e., righteousness), the capacity to act responsibly and fairly while living among groups of individuals within a society or community (i.e., social responsibility), a belief that you as an individual member of society do have the capacity to monitor and control events with the collective support of other group members (i.e., an inter-nal attributional system), and, finally, the capacity to share resources in an equitable manner and consider the needs of others above your own (i.e., low egocentrism) form the altruistic personality.

While current research has identified key personality traits as *evolved* mechanisms within both an egoistic and an altruistic perspective, a key factor to consider relative to community development is that cooperative behaviors and participation among interdependent activities can help shape behaviors to become less egoistic, intervene in emergency situations, and reduce environments that contribute to conflict and violence (Abbott & Cameron, 2014). Perhaps one reason why community development and service-related activities help reduce tendencies for aggression is that they promote an awareness of the needs of others and provide opportunities for individuals to collaborate and work toward mutually beneficial goals that support and strengthen our society.

Bierhoff, Klein and Kramp (1991) have theorized that the "altruistic personality" is really a combination of several traits:

1. **Empathy** (i.e., the capacity to both feel and understand what others may be experiencing). We are significantly more likely to intervene and help others if we have shared in (and experienced) the pain that other people (i.e., strangers) may be feeling. This is why groups that become polarized and isolated from real-world injustices need to be aware of the atrocities that exist. The capacity to feel what others may be feeling can also help to reduce the tendency to blame others (i.e., victim blaming) for their misfortunes. When individuals have been harmed and victimized themselves, in many situations, their reaction is a drive to end suffering by others because they have experienced the same kind of pain (Staub & Vollhardt, 2008). This psychological phenomenon is common among prisoners of war, who (despite being tortured) are proactive in their efforts to display forgiveness to their captors and those who have deliberately harmed them (Freedman & Zarifkar, 2016).

2. **Justice**. An altruistic individual believes (despite numerous cases of human exploitation) in a fair and just world, and that, ultimately, our actions are needed to help others who may have been victimized or oppressed. The altruist is neither naïve nor unassuming in that evil does not exist in some communities, but also recognizes that personal intervention is often required to help other individuals who may be incapable of defending themselves. An inherent belief in a fair, reasonable, and just world (i.e., good triumphs over evil) is fundamental to engagement in prosocial and altruistic behavior.

3. **Social responsibility**. Social responsibility refers to an awareness that in some situations, problems cannot be resolved individually. The altruistic individual has a unique capacity to motivate others simply through their own virtuous behavior. Additionally, the altruistic individual realizes that people need to work together and collectively to overcome serious problems such as oppression, discrimination, and hate crimes.

4. **Internal locus of control**. Locus of control refers to a belief whether or not we actually have control over the events that occur in our lives. Stanley Milgram (1974) and Phillip Zimbardo (2007) both discovered that when guards (and in some cases even prisoners themselves) become institutionalized (i.e., Nazi war crimes). Individuals who have become institutionalized justify their own inhumane treatment of others by convincing themselves that they have no control over their own actions (i.e., an external locus of control) and that they were simply "following orders" as a means of their own survival.

   During the infamous Nuremberg trials (*Die Nurnberger Prozesse*), several captured German officers claimed that the only justification for their heinous war crimes was that they were following orders from their military superior Adolf Hitler (e.g., Adolf Eichmann, who was later captured by the Israeli forces in Argentina and hanged in 1962).[4] In other situations, the guards justified their inhumane actions by claiming that the inmates and oppressed groups they were holding "deserved" their inhumane treatment because of their religion, ethnicity, or sexual identity. In essence, the guards renounced their own personal responsibility and culpability regarding war crimes by claiming that they lacked an internal locus of control and refused to take responsibility for their individual actions. In order to change and, ultimately, eradicate human war crimes (i.e., genocide), individuals *can and must* believe that they control their own destinies in making decisions that virtually mean life or death among innocent victims. The development of personal fortitude means individuals may make unpopular decisions among their peers and stand up for the rights of the persecuted, even risking their own personal freedom to do so.

5. **Low egocentrism**. The final requisite to the altruistic personality is in simply recognizing the needs of others and placing their needs above your own. While it may be true that all societies comprise a delicate balance between egoists and altruists, as recognized in the social contract theory (Cosmides & Tooby, 1992), cooperation among individuals living in groups and related practices (i.e., reciprocal altruism) are essential for improving living conditions among humans and their offspring (see Fig. 3.2).

---

[4] https://en.wikipedia.org/wiki/Nuremberg_trials.

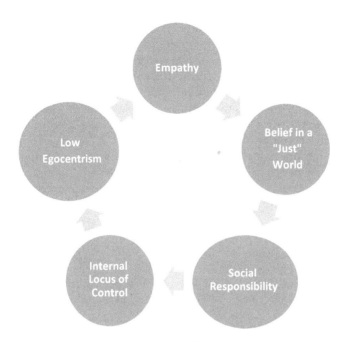

Fig. 3.2   The altruistic personality (Bierhoff, Klein, & Kramp, 1991)

Low egocentrism is considered to be an essential component to person-ality traits that are high in altruistic and prosocial behaviors because they are traits that direct attention of the individual to the needs of the group itself. Related characteristics that are commonly found within the altruistic individual, such as trust, cooperative behaviors, and a strong sense of con-nectedness to community, are necessary in that they serve as motivators and incentives to engage with and assist others who may need our assis-tance (McLeigh, 2015).

In an interesting article that addresses emotional affect such as grati-tude and well-being, Walker, Kumar and Gilovich (2016) compared the emotional effects (i.e., gratitude) of material consumption (i.e., purchas-ing things to help improve how we feel and combat depression) as opposed to what they refer to as "experiential" consumption—the opportunities for individuals not to purchase anything, but rather to actually experience an effect, similar to those found in a vacation or physical activity, such as hiking outdoors. The researchers found that *specific* forms of consumerism (i.e., those involving opportunities of aesthetic experiential processes) were significantly more likely to inspire gratitude and prosocial behaviors within various forms of green space environments. Additionally, Walker et al. (2016) surmised that because the consumption of positive experiences resulted in a type of euphoric "untargeted gratitude," combined with highly powerful positive feelings for others, there was an increased sense of reciprocity, which motivated individuals to give back to their community with a greater sense of collectivistic ideology. This increased sense of gratitude, which has been attributed by simply reflecting on positive experiential behaviors, has also been shown to be a necessary (but not sufficient) precursor to the existence of altruistic and prosocial behaviors (Bartlett & DeSteno, 2006).

REFERENCES

Abbott, N., & Cameron, L. (2014). What makes a young assertive bystander? The effect of intergroup contact, empathy, cultural openness, and in-group bias on assertive bystander intervention intentions. *Journal of Social Issues, 70*(1), 167–182.

Abu-Ras, W. M., & Suarez, E. Z. (2009). Muslim men and women's perception of discrimination, hate crimes and PTSD symptoms post 9/11. *Traumatology, 15*(3), 48–63.

Ainsworth, S. E., & Maner, J. K. (2012). Sex begets violence: Mating motives, social dominance, and physical aggression in men. *Journal of Personality and Social Psychology, 103*(5), 819–829.

Alaimo, K., Reischl, T. M., & Allen, J. O. (2010). Community gardening, neighborhood meetings, and social capital. *Journal of Community Psychology, 38*(4), 497–514.

Al-Ramiah, A., & Hewstone, M. (2013). Intergroup contact as a tool for reducing, resolving and preventing intergroup conflict. *American Psychologist, 68*(7), 527–542.

Archer, J. (2004). Sex differences in aggression in real-world settings: A meta-analytic review. *Review of General Psychology, 8*, 291–322.

Archer, J. (2013). Can evolutionary principles explain patterns of family violence? *Psychological Bulletin, 139*(2), 403–440.

Awad, G. H. (2010). The impact of acculturation and religious identification on perceived discrimination for Arab/Middle Eastern Americans. *Cultural Diversity and Ethnic Minority Psychology, 16*(1), 59–67.

Bandura, A. (1977). *Social learning theory.* Englewood Cliffs, NJ: Prentice-Hall.

Bank, L., & Barraston, B. (2001). Abusive home environments as predictors of poor adjustment during adolescence and early childhood. *Journal of Community Psychology, 29*, 195–217.

Bartlett, M. Y., & DeSteno, D. (2006). Gratitude and prosocial behavior: Helping when it costs you. *Psychological Science, 17*, 319–325.

Berry, J. W. (2013). Achieving a global psychology. *Canadian Psychology, 54*(1), 55–61.

Bierhoff, H. W., Klein, R., & Kramp, P. (1991). Evidence for the altruistic personality from data on accident research. *Journal of Personality, 59*, 263–280.

Bierhoff, H. W., & Rohmann, E. (2004). Altruistic personality in the context of the empathy-altruism hypothesis. *European Journal of Personality, 18*, 351–365.

Bushman, B. J., & Huesmann, L. R. (2013). Twenty-five years of research on violence in digital games and aggression revisited. *European Psychologist, 19*(1), 47–55.

Buss, D. M. (2005). *The murderer next door: Why the human mind is designed to kill.* New York: Penguin.

Buss, D. M. (2015). *Evolutionary psychology: The new science of the mind* (5th ed.). London: Pearson Publishers.

Buss, D. M., & Duntley, J. D. (2008). Adaptations for exploitation. *Group Dynamics, 12*, 53–62.

Buss, D. M., & Shackleford, T. K. (1997). Human aggression in evolutionary psychological perspective. *Clinical Psychology Review, 17*, 605–619.

Carlo, G., Eisenberg, N., Troyer, D., Switzer, G., & Speer, A. L. (1991). The altruistic personality: In what contexts is it apparent? *Journal of Personality and Social Psychology, 61*(3), 450–458.

Carter, R. T. (2007). Racism and psychological and emotional injury: Recognizing and assessing race-based traumatic stress. *The Counseling Psychologist, 35*, 13–105.

Cheesman, N. (2011). How an authoritarian regime in Burma used special courts to defeat judicial independence. *Law and Society Review, 45*(4), 801–830.

Chien, C. L. (2016, June 30). Beyond the authoritarian personality: The culture inclusive theory of Chinese orientation. *Frontiers in Psychology, 7*(924), 1–14.

Cosmides, L., & Tooby, J. (1992). Cognitive adaptations for social exchange. In J. Barkow, L. Cosmides, & J. Tooby (Eds.), *The adapted mind* (pp. 163–228). New York: Oxford University Press.

Dollard, J., Miller, N. E., Doob, L. W., Mowrer, O. H., & Sears, R. R. (1939). *Frustration aggression.* New Haven: Yale University Press.

Eggen, D. (2003, December 19). Tapes show abuse of 9/11 detainees: Justice Department examines videos prison officials said were destroyed. *The Washington Post*, p. A01.

Ferguson, C. J., & Kilburn, J. (2009). The public health risks of media violence: A meta-analytic review. *Journal of Pediatrics, 154*, 759–763.

Fiske, S. T. (2002). What we know now about bias and intergroup conflict, the problem of the century. *Current Directions in Psychological Science, 11*(4), 123–128.

Flook, L., Goldberg, S. B., Pinger, L., & Davidson, R. J. (2015). Promoting prosocial behavior and self-regulatory skills in preschool children through a mindfulness-based curriculum. *Developmental Psychology, 51*(1), 44–51.

Forbes, G., Zhang, X., Doroszewicz, K., & Haas, K. (2009). Relationships between individualism-collectivism, gender, and direct or indirect aggression: A study in China, Poland, and the US. *Aggressive Behavior, 35,* 24–30.

Freedman, S., & Zarifkar, T. (2016). The psychology of interpersonal forgiveness and guidelines for forgiveness therapy: What therapists need to know to help their clients forgive. *Spirituality in Clinical Practice, 3*(1), 45–58.

Goldsmith, B. (2014). http://uk.reuters.com/article/uk-britain-muslim-veils-idUKKBN0GL0X720140821

Goldstein, J. H. (1986). *Aggression and crimes of violence.* New York: Oxford University Press.

Green, A. H. (1998). Factors contributing to the generational transmission of child maltreatment. *Journal of American Academic of Child & Adolescent Psychiatry, 37*(12), 1334–1336.

Green, D. P., Glaser, J., & Rich, A. (1998). From lynching to Gay bashing: The elusive connection between economic conditions and hate crimes. *Journal of Personality and Social Psychology, 75*(1), 82–92.

Hamby, S. (2015). On the use of race and ethnicity as variables in violence research. *Psychology of Violence, 5*(1), 1–7.

Hanish, L. D., Sallquist, J., DiDonato, M., Fabes, R. A., & Martin, C. L. (2012). Aggression by whom – aggression toward whom: Behavioral Predictors of same- and other-gender aggression in early childhood. *Developmental Psychology, 48*(5), 1450–1462.

Hardaway, C. R., Larkby, C. A., & Cornelius, M. D. (2014). Socioemotional adjustment as a mediator of the association between exposure to community violence and academic performance in low-income adolescents. *Psychology of Violence, 4*(3), 281–2943.

Hardaway, C. R., Sterrett-Hong, E., Larkby, C. A., & Cornelius, M. D. (2016). Family resources as protective factors for low-income youth exposed to community violence. *Journal of Youth Adolescence, 45,* 1309–1322.

Helphand, K. (2006). *Defiant gardens: Making gardens in wartime.* San Antonio, TX: Trinity University Press.

Hennessy-Fisk, M. (2015 December 28). *After attacks, Muslim women say headscarves make them target* (p. 8A). Saint Paul: *St. Paul Pioneer Press.*

Hoffman, A. J. (2014). Build a fruit tree orchard and they will come: Creating an eco-identity via community gardening activities. *Community Development Journal, 50*(1), 104–120.

Hofstede, G. (1980). *Culture's consequences.* Beverly Hills, CA: Sage.

Hovland, C. I., & Sears, R. R. (1940). Minor studies of aggression: Correlation of lynchings with economic indices. *The Journal of Psychology, 9,* 301–310.

Huesmann, L. R. (2010). Nailing the coffin shut on doubts that violent video games stimulate aggression: Comment on Anderson, et al. (2010). *Psychological Bulletin, 136*(2), 179–181.

Huesmann, L. R., & Kirwil, L. (2007). Why observing violence increases the risk of violent behavior in the observer. In D. J. Flannery, A. T. Vazsonyi, & I. D. Waldman (Eds.), *The Cambridge handbook of violent behavior and aggression* (pp. 545–570). Cambridge: Cambridge University Press.

Ilmarinen, V. J., Vainikainen, M. P., Verkasalo, M., & Lonnqvist, J. E. (2015). Why are extroverts more popular? Oral fluency mediates the effect of extroversion on popularity in middle childhood. *European Journal of Personality, 29*, 138–151.

Latane, B., & Darley, J. B. (1968). Group inhibition of bystander intervention in emergencies. *Journal of Personality and Social Psychology, 10*, 308–324.

Machackova, H., & Pfetsch, J. (2016). Bystanders' responses to offline bullying and cyberbullying: The role of empathy and normative beliefs about aggression. *Scandinavian Journal of Psychology, 57*, 169–176.

McDonald, R., Jouriles, E. N., Ramisetty-Mikler, S., Caetano, R., & Green, C. E. (2006). Estimating the number of American children living in partner-violent families. *Journal of Family Psychology, 20*(1), 137–142.

McLeigh, J. D. (2015). Creating conditions that promote trust and participation by young people . . . and why it matters. *American Journal of Orthopsychiatry, 85*(6), S67–S69.

Milgram, S. (1974). *Obedience to authority: An experimental view*. New York, NY: Harper & Row.

Miller, P. A., & Eisenberg, N. (1988). The relation of empathy to aggressive and external/antisocial behavior. *Psychological Bulletin, 103*, 324–344.

Myers, M. (1998). Empowerment and community building through a gardening project. *Psychiatric Rehabilitation Journal, 22*(2), 181–183.

Nazzal, K. H., Forghany, M., Geevarughse, M. C., Mahmoodi, V., & Wong, J. (2014). An innovative community-oriented approach to prevention and early intervention with refugees in the United States. *Psychological Services, 11*(4), 477–485.

Negy, C., Shreve, T. L., Jensen, B. J., & Uddin, N. (2003). Ethnic identity, self-esteem, and ethnocentrism: A study of social identity versus multiculturalism theory of development. *Cultural Diversity and Ethnic Minority Psychology, 9*(4), 333–344.

Newton, E. K., Laible, D., Carlo, G., Steele, J. S., & McGinley, M. (2014). Do sensitive parents foster kind children, or vice-versa? Bidirectional influences between children's prosocial behavior and parental sensitivity. *Developmental Psychology, 50*(6), 1808–1816.

Parker, G. A. (2006). Sexual selection over mating and fertilization: An overview. *Philosophical Transactions of the Royal Society, B, 361*, 235–259.

Paschall, M. J., & Hubbard, M. L. (1998). Effects of neighborhood and family stressors on African-American male adolescents' self-worth and propensity for violent behavior. *Journal of Counseling and Clinical Psychology, 66*(5), 825–831.

Pelletier, L. G., Lavergne, K. J., & Sharp, E. C. (2008). Environmental psychology and sustainability: Comments on topics important for our future. *Canadian Psychology, 49,* 304–308.

Piff, P. K., Martinez, A. G., Stancato, D. M., Kraus, M. W., & Keltner, D. (2012). Class, chaos and the construction of community. *Journal of Personality and Social Psychology, 103*(6), 949–962.

Portes, A., & Rumbaut, R. G. (2006). *Immigrant America: A portrait.* Berkeley, CA: University of California Press.

Putnam, R. (2000). *Bowling alone: The collapse and revival of American community.* New York: Simon & Shuster.

Rosenthal, L., Levy, S. R., Katser, M., & Bazile, C. (2015). Polyculturalism and attitudes toward Muslim Americans. *Peace and Conflict: Journal of Peace Psychology, 21*(4), 535–545.

Ruiz, J. M., Gallardo, M. E., & Delgado-Romero, E. A. (2013). Latinas/os and immigration reform: A commentary to "Crossroads: The psychology of immigration in the new century" – The report of the APA presidential task force on immigration. *Journal of Latina/o Psychology, 1*(3), 149–154.

Ruiz, J. M., Steffen, P., & Smith, T. B. (2013). The Hispanic mortality paradox: A systematic review and meta-analysis of the longitudinal literature. *American Journal of Public Health, 103,* e52–e60.

Rutkowski, G. K., Gruder, C. L., & Romer, D. (1983). Group cohesiveness, social norms, and bystander intervention. *Journal of Personality and Social Psychology, 44*(3), 545–552.

Saad, L. (2006). *The Gallup Poll: Anti-Muslim sentiments fairly commonplace.* From http://www.gallup.com/poll/24073/antiMuslim-sentiments-fairly-commonplace.aspx

Schneider, W., Waldfogel, J., & Brooks-Gunn, J. (2015). The great recession and behavior problems in 9-year old children. *Developmental Psychology, 51*(11), 1615–1629.

Shan, H., & Walter, P. (2015). Growing everyday multiculturalism: Practice-based learning of Chinese immigrants through community gardens in Canada. *Adult Education Quarterly, 65,* 19–34.

Smith, P. K., & Myron-Wilson, R. (1998). Parenting and school bullying. *Clinical Child Psychology and Psychiatry, 3,* 405–417.

Sood, A. B., & Berkowitz, S. J. (2016). Prevention of youth violence: A public health approach. *Child and Adolescent Psychiatric Clinics of North America, 25*(2), 243–256.

Staerke, C., Clemence, A., & Doise, W. (1998). Representation of human rights across different National contexts: The role of democratic and non-democratic populations and generations. *European Journal of Social Psychology, 28,* 207–226.

Staub, E. (2005). The roots of goodness: The fulfillment of basic human needs and the development of caring, helping and nonaggression, inclusive caring, moral courage, active bystandership and altruism born of suffering. In G. Carlo & C. Edwards (Eds.), *Nebraska Symposium on Motivation: Vol. 51. Moral motivation through the life span: Theory, research and applications* (pp. 33–72). Lincoln: University of Nebraska Press.

Staub, E. (2013). Building a peaceful society: Origins, prevention, and reconciliation after genocide and other group violence. *American Psychologist, 68*(7), 576 589.

Staub, E., & Vollhardt, J. (2008). Altruism born of suffering: The roots of caring and helping after experiences of personal and political victimization. *American Journal of Orthopsychiatry, 78*, 267–280.

Ulug, O. M., & Cohrs, J. C. (2017). "If we become friends, maybe I can change my perspective:" Intergroup contact, endorsement of conflict narratives, and peace-related attitudes in Turkey. *Peace and Conflict: Journal of Peace Psychology, 23*(3), 278–287.

Uskul, A. K., & Over, H. (2017). Culture, social interdependence and ostracism. *Psychological Science, 26*(4), 371–376.

Van den Buick, J., Cetin, Y., Terzi, O., & Bushman, B. (2016). Violence, sex, and dreams: Violent and sexual media content infiltrate our dreams at night. *Dreaming, 26*(4), 271–279.

Velasco, G., & Dockterman, D. (2010). *Statistical portrait of Hispanics in the United States, 2008*. Washington, DC: Pew Hispanic Center.

Walker, J., Kumar, A., & Gilovich, T. (2016). Cultivating gratitude and giving through experiential consumption. *Emotion, 16*(8), 1126–1136.

Walter, P. (2013). Theorizing community gardens as pedagogical sites in the food movement. *Environmental Education Research, 19*(4), 521–539.

Weine, S. M. (2011, September). Developing preventative mental health interventions for refugee families in resettlement. *Family Processes, 50*, 410–430.

Zillman, D. (1971). Excitation transfer in communication-mediated aggressive behavior. *Journal of Experimental Social Psychology, 7*(4), 419–434.

Zimbardo, P. G. (2007). *The Lucifer effect: Understanding how good people turn evil*. New York, NY: Random House.

CHAPTER 4

Racial Constructs in Youth Mentoring: Reconsidering Race and Ethnicity

Youth mentoring has been enjoying a rapid growth in programs, research, and public support in the last few decades. What remains a critical question, especially given the political climate in the United States, is the role of race and ethnicity in youth mentoring relationships. Research on the influences of race and ethnicity in youth mentoring is in its infancy (Liang & Grossman, 2007; Park, Yoon, & Crosby, 2016; Weiston-Serdan, 2017), yet such work is critical for a number of reasons. First of all, researchers have recognized that not all mentoring relationships are effective and, in some cases, can do more harm than good (Rhodes, Liang, & Spencer, 2009). This knowledge, together with the explosion of youth mentoring programs across the country, has prompted researchers to explore the predictors of enduring and beneficial matches—from the mentor's competence to the mentor–mentee fit. Among these predictors, racial matching of mentoring pairs has been a question for youth mentoring programs, researchers, and consumers alike, since the majority of volunteer mentors in formal mentoring programs are White (77%), while those referred to these programs are often youth of color (Raposa, Dietz, & Rhodes, 2017; Rhodes, Reddy, Grossman, & Lee, 2002; Valentino & Wheeler, 2013). But beyond the demographics of program participants, race, ethnicity, and culture can influence youth's experiences in and out of the program (Fredricks & Simpkins, 2012).

© The Author(s) 2018   79
A. J. Hoffman et al., *The Role of Community Development in Reducing Extremism and Ethnic Conflict*,
https://Doi.org/10.1007/978-3-319-75699-8_4

It is important to note that race and ethnicity are distinct concepts, despite the fact that these terms are often used interchangeably (Liang, 2017; Williams & Deutsch, 2016). Race is a socially constructed classification of people based on physical criteria. Historically, race was determined by class inequities, but later was determined by skin color, where non-White people were afforded inferior privileges compared with White people. Ethnicity refers to one's group affiliations in a geographic region; group members may share some or all of their culture's practices (e.g., language, religion, norms, beliefs, values, customs). Sharing an ethnicity, however, does not necessitate sharing the same cultural beliefs and norms. For example, first-generation Chinese-Americans living in the United States may have very different cultural beliefs and norms than do their immigrant parents.

In general, developmental theories and positive youth development programs that recognize the importance of sociocultural context also recognize the importance of race and ethnicity given that these are grouping categories that reflect and encompass various sociocultural contexts (Williams & Deutsch, 2016). Thus, in the youth mentoring field, there has been some research into whether and how race matters when it comes to matching youth of color with mentors of the same racial or ethnic background. Firstly, proponents of same-race matches argue that mentors with a similar background may be better attuned to minority youth in a number of ways—that these mentors may be better able to understand the social and psychological conflicts of minority youth (Kalbfleisch & Davies, 1991), and may naturally share deeper levels of trust and cooperation, and thus may be more effective in helping them achieve their goals (Liang & Grossman, 2007; Sánchez & Colón, 2005). Secondly, proponents of same-race mentoring are concerned that mentors might struggle with "white guilt"—an assumption that when White mentors are confronted with the history of racial oppression, they might feel guilty and defensive in ways that keep them from being authentic in dealing with important issues such as race. Thirdly, studies of natural mentoring among adolescents and college-aged students suggest that minority mentors and mentees may prefer same-race matches. For example, Black mentors compared with White mentors more often initiated connections with Black mentees to play a role in their personal and professional development (Kalbfleisch & Davies, 1991). Many parents of youth also prefer having their children matched with a same-race mentor. Similarly, adolescents themselves tend to select role models and mentors who are of the same racial and ethnic background (Cavell, Meehan, Heffer, & Holladay, 2002; Jackson, Kite, & Branscombe, 1996; Sánchez & Colón, 2005). These findings raise the question of whether such preferences should be respected in formal mentoring programs.

On the other side of the debate, proponents of cross-race mentoring point to research that indicates that effective relationships can develop despite background differences; many in this camp view the racial difference as a crucible for relational growth. Some claim that cross-race matching, rather than being a disadvantage, can actually bridge social distances and challenge negative stereotypes (Rhodes et al., 2002). Even those who recognize the potentially important influences of mentor–mentee matches in culture and race are troubled by the bottom line—the relative dearth of minority mentors available. As such, matching by race may force scores of minority youth to wait on long waitlists until same-race volunteers become available (Diversi & Mecham 2005).

For all these reasons, researchers and practitioners should become critically informed about benefits of same-race versus cross-race matching. Yet, a singular focus on whether matching youth of color with same-race versus different-race mentors makes a difference is too simplistic. This chapter posits that more research is needed to uncover the complicated interplay between structural inequalities, interpersonal power, and the needs of mentees—many of whom are members of marginalized groups with marginalized social identities (e.g., racial/ethnic minorities, immigrants, low socioeconomic status). Indeed, such youth are reporting serious concerns and life challenges pertaining to shifts in policy and public discourse. Thus, it is important to bring attention to the complex needs and strengths that marginalized youth bring to bear in their mentoring relationships, as well as the needs to be supported in the development of their critical consciousness and racial and ethnic identity (Suyemoto, Day, & Schwartz, 2015). Moreover, research is needed to elucidate how mentors and mentees determine which inequalities are salient in their relationship, as well as define the meaning of these inequalities.

Youth mentoring research needs to go beyond using racial categories as a proxy for racial attitudes and beliefs. Racial categories are imprecise measures of actual psychological attitudes, beliefs, and experiences. When scholars use racial categories as independent variables to determine mentoring outcomes, they may inadvertently reify what are essentially racial stereotypes. Thus, building upon a previous review of the literature (Liang and Grossman, 2007), the current chapter provides an analysis of the relative benefits and costs of same-race versus cross-race relationships from three perspectives, as well as provides perspectives into extending considerations of race and ethnicity. Specifically, this chapter offers a critical review of the literature from three angles: (a) *outcomes*: examining the inconsistency and flaws of research that examines whether same-race matches are more beneficial than cross-race matches; (b) *process*: examining evidence for the role of racial constructs (e.g., racial stereotyping, racial identity) in the process of mentoring (e.g., the way mentors and mentees relate); (c) *application*: exploring how racial constructs might shape future research and practices.

OUTCOMES

Research in the mentoring field has tended to frame the question about whether race matters in terms of whether youth prefer or naturally gravitate toward mentors of the same racial or ethnic background, and whether same-race matches are associated with better outcomes than cross-race matches. Studies on formal mentoring programs comparing the benefits of same-race and cross-race matches have produced mixed findings. For example, Ensher and Murphy (1997) found that youth in same-race matches, compared with those in cross-race matches, reported receiving more instrumental support. Matching by race, however, was not associated with youth-reported levels of emotional support or youth's satisfaction with their mentors. Instead, this study suggested that mentees in cross-race matches might be just as satisfied as those in same-race matches if they perceive themselves to be similar to mentors in other ways. Moreover, in a study of 476 African American, Latino, American Indian, and Asian American youth, Rhodes and colleagues (2002) compared same-race and cross-race matches (where all cross-race mentors were White) in the Big Brothers Big Sisters national survey. Minority youth in the two groups did not differ on any of the 16 outcome variables at the beginning of the study. At the end of the study, only one group difference stood out: adolescents in same-race matches were somewhat more likely to report the initiation of alcohol use than adolescents in cross-race matches. Moreover, parents and guardians held slightly better impressions of cross-race relationships—they were more likely to report that the White mentors helped to build on their children's strengths, to improve their peer relationships, and to provide social and recreational opportunities. When matches were based on shared interests, geographic proximity, and youth and parental preferences for same-race pairs, cross-race pairs were just good as the same-race pairs in terms of frequency of meetings and duration of relationships.

In fact, youth in cross-race matches felt that they could more often "talk to their mentors" when things were bothering them and felt that they received more unconditional support. Some evidence suggests that such preferences for White mentors may have to do with racial identity status and unconscious bias among mentees and their parents. For example, African American youth with strong racial identities showed greater trust toward same-race mentors than toward White mentors, whereas those with weak racial identities were closer to White mentors (Linnehan, Weer, & Uhl, 2005).

Researchers in the field have at times taken these findings as support for cross-race matches, and at the least suggested that matching by race may not make a difference in mentoring outcomes (Rhodes et al., 2002). Indeed, such conclusions would provide relief for those concerned over the disproportionate number of minority mentees and mentors. Nevertheless, we caution that interpreting the outcome research this way may be misleading for a number of reasons, including the fact that outcome research may not be sensitive enough to detect the nuanced dynamics of mentoring relationships.

For example, in a study by Spencer, Basualdo-Delmonico, and Lewis (2011), several parents of color wished for a same-race match but did not express this desire to the agency for a variety of reasons. These reasons included preferring a match over having their child stay on the waiting list and believing that they should privilege character traits over race, despite a strong sense that a same-race mentor may be easier to relate to, and may be a more relevant role model for their child. One parent saw how much her child was getting from his relationship with a White mentor, in terms of gifts and opportunities, and so despite her discomfort about accepting these "handouts" from a "wealthier mentor," she did not want her child to be deprived of all he was getting out of this relationship. Although these parents were pleased that mentoring had afforded their children access to new opportunities and experiences, their narratives shine a light on some of the complicated and ambivalent feelings parents may bear when mentors of more privileged racial and social class backgrounds enter into the life of their child and family. These are ambivalences that are not readily picked up in the quantitative outcome research.

Moreover, the great majority of the extant quantitative findings on youth mentoring have been reported from secondary analyses of larger studies that were designed to answer non-race–related research questions. In other words, the data of these studies were not collected to explicitly assess the impact of race and ethnicity, and thus leave out variables that may have more relevance to race and ethnicity. Studies that found no differences or even advantages in cross-race matches used outcome variables such as emotional/ psychological problems, problem behavior, self-esteem, social competence, academic achievement, career/employment success, and satisfaction with mentoring relationship (Ensher & Murphy, 1997; Rhodes et al., 2002).

Cultural factors have rarely been included as outcome variables, and there is little evidence that cultural considerations have been explicitly integrated into the frequently used outcome variables in youth mentoring research and positive youth development research. Thus, the question remains as to whether there would be differences in same-race versus cross-race matches when considering outcomes more directly relevant to race, ethnicity, and culture, such as racial identity development, cultural trust versus mistrust, receptiveness to critical feedback, acculturation, and navigating biculturalism? Given that the conventional outcome instruments measure success and well-being as defined by the Eurocentric context in which they were developed, it can be argued that they tend to be a reflection of the degree to which mentees of color have "become white" with the help of White mentors. That is, because these outcome instruments are typically developed in Eurocentric contexts, they may be, in a sense, indices of "how *white* minority mentees fair with the help of their white mentors" or "degree of success by white definitions and standards."

The limited research that exists on culturally relevant outcomes suggests that same-race adults, compared with different-race adults, are more capable of guiding youth in coping with stereotypes and social barriers they might face. Moreover, minority mentors are more empathic and offer more realistic coping strategies to their same-race mentees, especially when it comes to dealing with social barriers such as racial discrimination (Park et al., 2016). Youth in same-race mentoring relationships had better self-concepts and a greater understanding of the importance of racial identity (Holland, 1996; Park et al., 2016).

Most importantly, scholars have pointed out that racial categories should not be used as a proxy for measuring an underlying racial construct (e.g., racial identity), since doing so perpetuates the myth that race or ethnicity has been measured (Helms, Jernigan, & Mascher, 2005). Assigning youth and their mentors to racial categories reveals more about the researchers' beliefs about race than about the actual attributes of the research participants. Instead, what is needed is statistical analyses of theory-derived variables to determine whether it matters to match mentors and mentees by similarities measured by racial constructs that actually reflect research participants' beliefs and attitudes. In other words, youth mentoring outcome research examining same-race versus cross-race matching should not be taken at face value. Instead, we need to consider the underlying racial construct qualities and processes that make mentoring transformative.

PROCESS

Research illuminating the relational processes in mentoring suggests that ethnicity and race play a role in the ways that mentors and mentees relate to each other (Liang, Tracy, Kauh, Taylor, & Williams, 2006). That is, the quality of mentoring relationships may be shaped by the way race- and culture-related issues are negotiated by mentor–mentee pairs. Below, we discuss four specific ways in which culture- and race-related issues may impinge on mentoring relationships: collectivistic versus individualistic values, cultural sensitivity, perceived similarity, and cultural mistrust.

First, research suggests that youth from collectivist backgrounds may be more comfortable seeking out and working with multiple mentors who are members of their own extended family, while youth from individualistic backgrounds may be more open to one-to-one relationships with adults outside the family (Liang & Grossman, 2007). Second, the quality of relationships and whether youth initially form relationships successfully are also affected by the degree of mentors' cultural sensitivity. For example, Liang et al. (2006) found that Asian college women, despite their strong interest in mentoring relationships, appeared to be less likely than non-Asians to initiate and express this interest openly due to cultural differences in emotional expression and attempts to communicate respectful boundaries—qualities that are heightened in the hierarchical relationships of Asians. Mentors who are insensitive to these cultural characteristics may be less apt to recognize a young Asian person's interest in the mentoring relationship and reciprocate interest.

This reciprocation of interest is important because voluntary mentoring relationships have been likened to love relationships (Liang et al., 2006) in that they rely on mutual selection and chemistry. In regard to mutual selection, literature suggests that mentors and mentees tend to hold different criteria. When mentors initiate these relationships, it is often because mentees have successfully attracted them through interpersonal skills or communication competence and expressions of interest. When mentees initiate, however, they are drawn to mentors from same-race/ethnic backgrounds, not to mention same gender. This may be due to the fact that perceived similarity has been associated with initial attraction. On the other hand, some researchers have conceptualized shared race as "surface-level" similarity, and shared interests, values, and personality as "deep-level" similarity—arguing that the latter matters more than the former once the relationship has had some time to develop (Ortiz-Walters & Gilson, 2005). Race may play a big role in the initial perceived similarity as a visible marker in this highly racialized society where there is a system of privilege based on skin color.

Fourth, Claude Steele (1997) identified stereotype threat and cultural mistrust as important influences on relationships between Blacks and Whites. The quality of mentoring relationships is also affected by the degree of cultural mistrust of the mentee, and how feedback is provided to the mentee (Cohen, Steele, & Ross, 1999; Sánchez & Colón, 2005). For example, in an experimental study, when a White evaluator gave Black and White college students critical feedback, the Black students rated the evaluator as more biased and were less motivated to revise their work. The Black students might have thought that they were judged on the basis of race rather than merit. However, the difference in perception and motivation between White and Black students disappeared when students were also informed that high standards were being used and were assured that the mentor believed they could meet those standards (Cohen et al., 1999). Indeed, the meaning of race and ethnicity is deeply embedded within a particular historical and cultural context. In the United States, mentoring relationships form in a context and society that hosts a legacy of discrimination against persons of color. This study shows how important it is for mentors to learn to give feedback in a way that is encouraging rather than discouraging.

Beyond Power Differentials and Racial Matching

Understanding the influence of race and ethnicity requires that scholars add complexity to the research questions and methods currently employed in youth mentoring studies that examine these constructs. Research must be done to examine how race and structural inequalities influence marginalized youth, as well as mentoring relationships. First, the meaning of race for individuals does not always replicate broader structures of inequality (Helms et al., 2005). Positionality refers to the state of being in a particular position in relation to other people, depending on a complexity of cultural values and social positions. Rather than considering positionality as fixed, Anthias (2002) posits that individuals experience and enact positionality in ways that may vary across social contexts (Anthias, 2002). Individuals cannot be reduced to their social locations and identifications, which are always in flux.

Indeed, the meaning of race for individuals is not only imposed from outside the mentoring relationship but can emerge through interaction between mentors and mentees. For example, Schippers' (2008) study of a mentoring program for Black youth demonstrated that these mentees held the power to make race salient, and even more importantly, to define racial difference as a status hierarchy that put blackness above whiteness. More specifically, the mentees in this study ignored the White mentors, and listened to the Black mentors. Not surprisingly, this hierarchy had a profound impact on the relationships between the mentors and the mentees—the Black mentors enjoyed their mentoring relationships far more than did the White mentors.

Taken together, research suggests the need for a more nuanced way of understanding how race and ethnicity affect youth and their mentoring relationships. It is important to recognize that youth's experiences are shaped by the interaction between their cultural contexts and social categories that may include and go beyond race and ethnicity.

Conclusion

In sum, mentoring outcome research has produced mixed results. The results have often been interpreted to mean that race and ethnicity do *not* play a definitive role in youth mentoring outcomes. While there are cases in which same-race matches are associated with better outcomes, in other cases, cross-race matches do just as well or better. These findings should be interpreted with a grain of salt because of the small effect sizes and because the outcomes measured do not tend to include race and culture variables (Grossman & Rhodes, 2002). Moreover, this body of literature points to the fact that high-quality mentoring programs tend to yield higher effect sizes. Yet, little research has explicitly revealed what, in fact, leads to quality, close relationships.

Still needed is process-oriented research that focuses on what happens in effective mentoring relationships that honor issues of race, ethnicity, and culture. The few quantitative studies that focus on process reveal that race and culture can make a difference in the ways that mentors and mentees relate. This research brings to light how insensitivity toward race and culture can lead to problematic relationships. Indeed, mentors need ongoing training and support to better understand and relate to mentees of diverse backgrounds (Weiston-Serdan, 2017). A culturally sensitive mentor with an understanding of the youth's values and worldview is critical to successful communication and connection. Along these lines, we need to also examine macro-level influences on the mentoring relationship such as race-related stereotypes that can affect mentors and, ultimately, the way they treat their mentees (Williams & Deutsch, 2016).

At the same time, we need to move beyond overly simplifying explanations of race, culture, and power that assume structural inequality as consistently behaving in a certain direction. There is an implicit assumption in this field that mentors, especially White mentors, hold all power over mentees. It does not recognize the dynamic influence of mentees in shaping power dynamics and other aspects of interactions. Indeed, Schippers' (2008) study demonstrated that navigating racial differences is not always the mechanism by which the larger structure is reproduced, but can also be the process by which the larger structure is usurped.

More qualitative and mixed-methods research is needed to reveal the more complicated interplay between structural inequalities, interpersonal power, and how mentors and mentees not only determine which inequalities are going to be salient in their relationship, but also define the meaning of these inequalities.

REFERENCES

Anthias, F. (2002). Where do I belong? Narrating collective identity and translocational positionality. *Ethnicities, 2*, 491–514.

Cavell, T. A., Meehan, B. T., Heffer, R. W., & Holladay, J. J. (2002). The natural mentors of adolescent children of alcoholics (COAs): Implications for preventive practices. *The Journal of Primary Prevention, 23*(1), 23–42. https://doi.org/10.1023/A:1016587115454.

Cohen, G. L., Steele, C. M., & Ross, L. D. (1999). The mentor's dilemma: Providing critical feedback across the racial divide. *Personality and Social Psychology Bulletin, 25*, 1302–1318.

Diversi, M., & Mecham, C. (2005). Latino(a) students and Caucasian mentors in a rural after-school program: Towards empowering adult-youth relationships. *Journal of Community Psychology, 33*(1), 31–40. https://doi.org/10.1002/jcop.20034.

Ensher, E., & Murphy, S. (1997). Effects of race, gender, perceived similarity, and contact on mentor relationships. *Journal of Vocational Behavior, 50*, 460–481.

Fredricks, J. A., & Simpkins, S. D. (2012). Promoting positive youth development through organized after-school activities: Taking a closer look at participation of ethnic minority youth. *Child Development Perspectives, 6*(3), 280–287. https://doi.org/10.1111/j.1750-8606.2011.00206.x.

Grossman, J. B., & Rhodes, J. E. (2002). The test of time: Predictors and effects of duration in youth mentoring relationships. *American Journal of Community Psychology, 30*, 199–219.

Helms, J. E., Jernigan, M., & Mascher, J. (2005). The meaning of race in psychology and how to change it: A methodological perspective. *American Psychologist, 60*(1), 27–36. https://doi.org/10.1037/0003-066X.60.1.27.

Holland, S. H. (1996). PROJECT 2000: An educational mentoring and academic support model for inner-city African American boys. *The Journal of Negro Education, 65*, 315–321.

Jackson, C. H., Kite, M. E., & Branscombe, N. R. (1996, August). *African-American women's mentoring experiences.* Paper presented at annual meeting of the American Psychological Association, Toronto, Canada. (ERIC Document Reproduction Service No. ED 401 371).

Kalbfleisch, P. J., & Davies, A. D. (1991). Minorities and mentoring: Managing the multicultural institution. *Communication Education, 40*, 266–271.

Liang, B. (2017). Race and ethnicity in out-of-school learning. In K. Peppler (Ed.), *The SAGE encyclopedia of out-of-school learning.* Thousand Oaks, CA: Sage Publications.

Liang, B., & Grossman, J. M. (2007). Diversity and youth mentoring. In T. D. Allen & L. T. Eby (Eds.), *The Blackwell handbook of mentoring: A multiple perspectives approach* (pp. 239–258). Oxford, England: Blackwell. https://doi. org/10.1002/9780470691960.ch152007-00535-015.

Liang, B., Tracy, A., Kauh, T., Taylor, C., & Williams, L. (2006). Mentoring Asian and Euro-American college women. *Journal of Multicultural Counseling and Development, 34*, 143–154.

Linnehan, F., Weer, C., & Uhl, J. (2005). African-American students' early trust beliefs in work-based mentors. *Journal of Vocational Behavior, 66*, 501–515.

Ortiz-Walters, R., & Gilson, L. L. (2005). Mentoring in academia: An examination of the experiences of protégés of color. *Journal of Vocational Behavior, 67*, 459–475.

Park, H., Yoon, J., & Crosby, S. D. (2016). A pilot study of big brothers big sisters programs and youth development: An application of critical race theory. *Children and Youth Services Review, 61*, 83–89. https://doi.org/10.1016/j. childyouth.2015.12.010.

Raposa, E. B., Dietz, N., & Rhodes, J. E. (2017). Trends in volunteer mentoring in the United States: Analysis of a decade of census survey data. *American Journal of Community Psychology, 1*, 1–12.

Rhodes, J., Liang, B., & Spencer, R. (2009). First do no harm: Ethical guidelines for youth mentoring relationships. *Professional Psychology, 40*, 452–458.

Rhodes, J. E., Reddy, R., Grossman, J. B., & Lee, J. M. (2002). Volunteer mentoring relationships with minority youth: An analysis of same- versus cross-race matches. *Journal of Applied Social Psychology, 32*(10), 2114–2133. https://doi. org/10.1111/j.1559-1816.2002.tb02066.x.

Sánchez, B., & Colón, Y. (2005). Race, ethnicity, and culture in mentoring relationships. In D. L. DuBois & M. J. Karcher (Eds.), *Handbook of youth mentoring* (pp. 191–204). Thousand Oaks, CA: Sage Publications. 10.4135/9781412976664.n13 2005-09468-013.

Schippers, M. (2008). Doing difference/doing power: Negotiations of race and gender in a mentoring program. *Symbolic Interaction, 31*(1), 77–98. https:// doi.org/10.1525/si.2008.31.1.77.

Spencer, R., Basualdo-Delmonico, A., & Lewis, T. O. (2011). Working to make it work: The role of parents in the youth mentoring process. *Journal of Community Psychology, 39*(1), 51–59.

Steele, C. M. (1997). A threat in the air: How stereotypes shape intellectual identity and performance. *American Psychologist, 52*(6), 613–629.

Suyemoto, K. L., Day, S. C., & Schwartz, S. (2015). Exploring effects of social justice youth programming on racial and ethnic identities and activism for Asian American youth. *Asian American Journal of Psychology, 6*(2), 125–135. https://doi.org/10.1037/a0037789.

Valentino, S., & Wheeler, M. (2013). *Big brothers big sisters report to America: Positive outcomes for a positive future. 2013 youth outcomes report*. Retrieved online from http://www.bbbs-gc.org/Websites/bbbsgallatincounty/images/ 20130425_BBBSA_YOS2013.pdf

Weiston-Serdan, T. (2017). *Critical mentoring: A practical guide.* Sterling, VA: Stylus Publishing.

Williams, J. L., & Deutsch, N. L. (2016). Beyond between-group differences: Considering race, ethnicity, and culture in research on positive youth development programs. *Applied Developmental Science, 20*(3), 203–213. https://doi.org/10.1080/10888691.2015.1113880.

CHAPTER 5

Cultural Perspectives on Ethnic Diversity and Social Capital and Intergroup Relations in Diverse Communities

Recent global immigration trends indicate that many Western societies will continue to diversify. Both Europe and the United States, for instance, have experienced net increases in migration rates, and it is estimated that one in ten persons is an immigrant in developed societies (Elliott, Mayadas, & Segal, 2010). Since 1965, the United States has received an estimated 59 million immigrants, resulting in a relatively high foreign-born population rate of 14% that is reshaping the ethnic/racial[1] landscape of and adding further complexity to race relations (Pew Research Center, 2015; Oliver & Ha, 2008). Other Western societies are experiencing social challenges as a result of similar, though less dramatic demographic shifts. These trends require us to think critically about intergroup relations, coexistence, cooperation (Maly, 2005), or social capital and also require answers to the following questions: *What leads to the success and failure of diverse communities? What facilitates or impedes social capital and intergroup relations among diverse groups?*

Answers to these questions are critical because of the historical and recent challenges associated with diversity (e.g., Bonilla-Silva, 2000). For instance, although a large number of Americans believe that immigrants

---

[1] Although there are distinctions between *ethnicity* and *race*, the two will be used interchangeably in the present chapter. *Ethnicity* will be used for the most part, as it is perhaps less controversial than *race*. *Ethnicity* refers to group membership based on a shared common social, cultural, and linguistic heritage, and ancestry (Berry, 2006a).

© The Author(s) 2018
A. J. Hoffman et al., *The Role of Community Development in Reducing Extremism and Ethnic Conflict*,
https://doi.org/10.1007/978-3-319-75699-8_5

are improving US society (45%), a sizable number believe that they are making it worse (37%; Pew Research Center, 2015). Similarly, in the United States, Europe, and other Western countries, diversity has been empirically shown to result in reduced social capital[2]—mostly, sense of community and social cohesion (e.g., Neal & Watling Neal, 2014; Putnam, 2001; Townley, Kloos, Green, & Franco, 2011; van der Meer & Tolsma, 2014; Veit, 2015). This recent scholarship parallels dominant and long-standing societal narratives on the putative negative effects of diversity and immigration on the broader social order (mostly in Western societies).[3] A negative societal consequence of such narratives is clearly observed in the rise of anti-immigrant and -diversity narratives in US and European society (see, e.g., the rise of US hate groups: www.splcenter.org).

Both the public and academia have primarily focused on the negative role that ethnic diversity has on social capital as well as on intergroup relations at the expense of broader, potential ultimate factors, giving credence to the notion that ethnic diversity is harmful to Western society. This is rather unfortunate, as ostensible ethnic conflict is not necessarily ethnic in origin or nature and is rare (see Landis & Albert, 2012). Conflicts typically involve a complex of factors and are historical in nature (e.g., Albert, Gabrielsen, & Landis, 2012; Landis & Albert, 2012). For instance, Pettigrew, Wagner, and Christ (2010) identified various macro-level factors that can negatively affect intergroup relations (specifically group threat and prejudice) and contribute to ethnic conflict. These include: (a) history of relations; (b) rapid increases in the size of a particular out-group faction; (c) social, legal, and political barriers to assimilation and citizenship; (d) multiple and salient differences between an in-group and an out-group; and (e) economic problems and perceived competition. These and other factors have been identified as influential in the backlash against multiculturalism in Europe (e.g., Koopmans, 2013).

---

[2] Although complex, multifaceted, and problematic in several ways, social capital has commonly been defined as the characteristics and resources that exist among networks of individuals (Cheong, Edwards, Goulbourne, & Solomos, 2007; Putnam, 2007; Portes & Vickstrom, 2011; van der Meer & Tolsma, 2014).

[3] Although diversity and immigration are distinct (Lancee & Schaeffer, 2015; Laurence & Heath, 2008; Putnam, 2007), both anti-diversity and anti-immigrant attitudes and sentiment are characterized by negative societal reactions regarding cultural differences, ethnocultural marginalization and rationalization of inequality, and resulting strong sense of nationalism (Bonilla-Silva, 2004).

Thus, a focus on ethnicity alone at the expense of cultural as well as ecological factors is unjustified and problematic (e.g., Laurence, 2011; Laurence & Heath, 2008). For one, culture is an important aspect of individuals lives, culture and cultural values serve as guiding principles, apparent individual- and societal-level differences in cultural characteristics and values matter[4], and culture (as well as cultural sensitivity) matter in our interconnected world (Alamilla, Scott, & Hughes, 2016; Fischer, 2014; House, 2004; Javidan, House, & Dorfman, 2004). Scholars from different traditions have noted that cultural proximity or concurrence will facilitate intercultural relations as well as immigrant adaptation and is an influential factor in the formation of mutual intergroup attitudes (e.g., Berry, 2006a). For instance, groups vary with respect to religiosity as a function of culture,[5] and religious differences appear to be related to harmonious or conflictual intergroup relations (Berry, 2006a). Yet cultural factors have largely been excluded from the ethnic diversity and social capital literature.

Similarly, despite the harmful effects of residential ethnic segregation (e.g., Massey & Denton, 1993; Williams & Collins, 2002a, 2002b), particularly to intergroup relations (Oliver, 2010; van der Meer & Tolsma, 2014), the social capital literature has not adequately assessed its impact on social capital. Neighborhood disadvantage, ethnic segregation, as well as other harmful neighborhood factors and conditions in and of themselves negatively impact social capital and intergroup relations (e.g., Cheong et al., 2007; Laurence, 2011; Laurence & Heath, 2008; Oliver & Ha, 2008). Unfortunately, because ethnic minorities are more likely to live in such neighborhoods, it may appear that ethnic diversity is solely responsible for any diminished levels of social capital and related problems.

Although the present work acknowledges the role of other, perhaps more proximal and/or potent factors in the relationship between ethnic diversity and social capital (e.g., racism, economic disadvantage, and inequality; global economic changes and global migration; Laurence & Heath, 2008; van der Meer & Tolsma, 2014), it focuses on the role of

---

[4] The greater the cultural differences between groups during the intercultural adaptation process, the greater the difficulties in intergroup relations as well as for the acculturating individual (Berry, 2006a, 2000b).

[5] Research has found that in-group collectivistic practices and values are significantly positively associated with religiosity (religious devotion and centrality) at the societal level (Gelfand, Bhawuk, Nishi, & Bechtold, 2004).

cultural factors because they have been undertheorized and understudied. Understanding how cultural factors might impact social capital may clarify the ethnic diversity and social capital literature as well as inform practice, largely because culture and ethnicity have often been conflated by researchers (e.g., Alamilla et al., 2016; Castillo & Caver, 2009). The significance of cultural factors (i.e., perceived differences) to intergroup relations is highlighted by social commentators Noam Chomsky and David Barsamian:

> There has always been racism ... When you have your boot on someone's neck, you have to justify it. The justification has to be their depravity. It's very striking to see this in the case of people who aren't very different from one another [referring to the British conquest and oppression of the Irish]. The Irish were a different race. They weren't human. They weren't like us. We had to crush them. (1994, pp. 64–65)

Purpose and Goals of Chapter

The present chapter is primarily concerned with providing a deeper understanding of the relationship between ethnic diversity and social capital as well as intergroup relations in the United States.[6] A major goal of the current chapter is to conceptually disentangle ethnic and cultural diversity from each other as well as from broader contextual factors (e.g., neighborhood disadvantage) and to highlight the potential benefits of addressing cultural factors to the analysis of ethnic diversity and social capital as well as intergroup relations. This work is critical, as the United States and other Western societies are experiencing societal challenges— ostensibly due to increasing diversity. In recent years, immigrants and ethnic minorities have become the objects of fear, blame, and scapegoating by their current societies, and nativism as well as anti-minority and immigrant groups have increased (Amnesty International, 2017; Cheong et al., 2007; Human Rights Watch, 2017). These troubling processes, which can be traced to broader social forces and to distant points in time, particularly the cultural nature of contemporary forms of racism (Bonilla-Silva, 2000), threaten democracy and human rights values (Roth, 2017)—

---

[6] The current chapter may have implications for other Western societies; however, scholars have pointed out the uniqueness of the United States with respect to ethnic diversity and social cohesion (e.g., van der Meer & Tolsma, 2014).

both of which are vital to social capital (Saegert, Thompson, & Warren, 2001; Sullivan, Snyder, & Sullivan, 2008).

Scope and Definitions The current work will focus on social capital and related constructs such as social cohesion as well as intergroup relations and attitudes in the United States.[7] Although defined in different and, at times, competing ways (Saegert & Carpiano, 2017), social capital refers to the properties of social relationships and networks (e.g., Portes, 1998; Putnam, 2007). Perhaps the most popular conceptualization and definition of social capital is Putnam's (2000), which defines it as the "social networks and the associated norms of reciprocity and trustworthiness" (Putnam, 2007, p. 137). Social capital is a multidimensional construct that consists of inclusionary as well as exclusionary aspects (Warren, Thompson, & Saegert, 2001), such as bridging social capital, which involves ties among individuals who are dissimilar, and bonding social capital, which involves ties among individuals who are similar (Putnam, 2007). Social capital may involve political associations and activities as well as non-political associations and activities (Putnam, 2007; Warren et al., 2001). Lastly, social capital is not uniformly beneficial to the larger society, as when criminal groups engage in illicit activities for the benefit of their group at the expense of others (Putnam, 2000, 2007; Warren et al., 2001).

Culture refers to the shared ideas, including religion and political ideology, practices, norms, and patterns of social relations and relationships (e.g., individualism and collectivism) associated with a particular society (House & Javidan, 2004; Kitayama, Duffy, & Uchida, 2007). There are two related constructs that capture individual-level changes as a result of intercultural or intergroup contact (Alamilla et al., 2016). Psychological acculturation refers to the process by which individual changes in knowledge, behaviors, values, and cultural identity occur as a result of such contact (Kim & Abreu, 2001), whereas enculturation refers to the process by which individuals are (re)socialized to traditional or indigenous cultural norms, that is, values, behaviors, attitudes, or worldviews (Kim & Abreu, 2001). As noted in Kim and Alamilla (2017), enculturation is an important construct not only for migrants but for ethnic minorities as well as those who have experienced colonialism.

---

[7] Although this chapter focuses primarily on scholarship conducted primarily in the United States, it will also draw on relevant scholarship from other Western societies.

NEIGHBORHOOD DIVERSITY AND SOCIAL CAPITAL

Despite strong claims made by some scholars (e.g., Putnam, 2007), the evidence on neighborhood diversity and social capital is mixed (Koopmans, Lancee, & Schaeffer, 2015; van der Meer & Tolsma, 2014).[8] Some consistent themes have emerged. These consist of moderating effects of diversity, impact of immigration versus diversity, as well as geographical level of analysis (e.g., within vs. between neighborhoods; Laurence & Heath, 2008; Oliver, 2010; Oliver & Ha, 2008; van der Meer & Tolsma, 2014). Perhaps the most surprising finding or trend concerns the beneficial effects of certain measures of neighborhood diversity on certain dimensions of social capital, such as community cohesion and more favorable intergroup attitudes (Koopmans et al., 2015; Laurence, 2011; Laurence & Heath, 2008; Oliver & Ha, 2008; Pettigrew & Tropp, 2006). Furthermore, ethnic diversity does not create negative intergroup relations and is unrelated to some dimensions of social capital (e.g., civic engagement; Putnam, 2007). As the literature clearly indicates, the association between diversity and social capital is not straightforward (e.g., Koopmans et al., 2015; van der Meer & Tolsma, 2014) and diversity may offer several short- and long-term benefits to society (see Putnam, 2007).

Using data from the Social Capital Community Benchmark Survey (SCCBS; 2000), Putnam (2007) found that ethnic diversity leads to social isolation and withdrawal among both majority- and minority-group members—that is, "hunkering down." This observation has been labeled *constrict theory* and refers to the negative effects of ethnic diversity on bridging and bonding social capital.[9] Typically, bivariate correlations have indicated a negative association between community-level ethnic diversity (measured with US Census tract[10]) and solidarity, trust, altruism, community cooperation, and friendships, that is, attitudinal, behavioral, bridging, bonding, public, as well as private dimensions of social capital (van der

---

[8] Although "neighborhoods" typically refer to relatively small geographical or areal units defined administratively (e.g., US Census Bureau block groups; Diez Roux, 2003, 2007), I will use this term and "community" interchangeably unless a specific work referenced has operationalized neighborhood differently (e.g., US Census Bureau tract or county). Note, van der Meer and Tolsma (2014) found mixed support for diversity and social cohesion.

[9] This is in contrast to the *contact hypothesis*, which maintains and has empirically demonstrated that diversity is beneficial and leads to positive social outcomes (e.g., Allport, 1954; Pettigrew & Tropp, 2006).

[10] Using a community ethnic diversity index, the mean Herfindahl index, which gives the likelihood that any two randomly selected individuals will be from the same group.

Meer & Tolsma, 2014). Similar findings were also reported for community-level immigration (measured with US Census county) using data collected by Rupasingha, Goetz, and Freshwater (2006). Despite these findings, some have questioned the claims of the robustness of constrict theory based on bivariate relationships (e.g., van der Meer & Tolsma, 2014; also see Dawkins, 2008 for theoretical and methodological critiques). Furthermore, the geographical unit of analysis matters (Oliver, 2010; Oliver & Ha, 2008; van der Meer & Tolsma, 2014). For instance, Oliver and Ha (2008) argue that the negative association between diversity measured at larger geographical units and social outcomes is attributed to increased competition for jobs, consistent with conflict theory. These issues notwithstanding, Putnam acknowledges the inherent benefits of ethnic diversity and its likely long-term benefits to American society.

Other scholars have made similar observations regarding the negative association between diversity and sense of community or bonding social capital (Neal & Watling Neal, 2014; Portes & Vickstrom, 2011; Townley et al., 2011). These findings are consistent with empirical work (e.g., Alesina, Baqir, & Easterly, 1999; Alesina & Ferrara, 2000; Costa & Kahn, 2003; Neal & Watling Neal, 2014) mostly theoretically grounded on homophily or the notion that *similarity* is conducive to bonding (McPherson, Smith-Lovin, & Cook, 2001). For instance, in a simulated study of 500 neighborhoods (as opposed to actual neighborhoods),[11] Neal and Watling Neal found that more diverse (integrated) neighborhoods had a lower sense of community (lower personal network density). Similarly, less diverse (more segregated) neighborhoods were more likely to have a higher sense of community (denser personal networks). However, one set of findings suggested that diversity and sense of community were compatible in settings that afforded proximity and ethnic heterophily. Because the level of geography and social capital are not independent (e.g., Oliver & Ha, 2008; van der Meer & Tolsma, 2014) and because sense of community is related to the size of a particular setting (Neat & Watling Neal, 2014), it is unclear whether these results are robust across different geographical areas. Importantly, these models assume, among other things, that networks are dependent on ethnic homophily and physical proximity, and only provide a correlation. They do not address more complex relationships involving different forms of homophily (e.g., value).

---

[11] This study utilized agent-based modeling and used a dissimilarity index to derive integrated versus segregated neighborhoods.

A more nuanced perspective on the relationship was provided by van der Meer and Tolsma (2014) in their review of 90 studies on ethnic diversity and social cohesion in several societies. These authors found that ethnic diversity was not unilaterally associated with decreased social cohesion. In fact, a substantial number of studies (n = 39) found mixed support for constrict theory. Furthermore, results depended on factors such as the formal versus informal dimension of social cohesion, attitudinal versus behavioral dimension of social cohesion, subject/object (e.g., in-group vs. out-group), and geographical unit of analysis (as well as bounded vs. generalized aspects of social cohesion). For instance, the positive association between ethnic diversity and social cohesion is most robust for informal and attitudinal, as opposed to formal and behavioral, dimensions. Yet van der Meer and Tolsma cautioned that there are just as many studies in support of constrict theory vis-à-vis the attitudinal dimension as there are against it. The literature is equivocal with regard to the impact of ethnic diversity and social cohesion for in-group versus out-group members. In fact, some studies consistently provided evidence against constrict theory for members of minority groups (e.g., Koopmans & Veit, 2013) and, in some cases, found increased intraethnic contact among minority groups, lending support for social psychological perspectives on the benefits of intergroup contact. Lastly, van der Meer and Tolsma found strong evidence for constrict theory for intraneighborhood social cohesion, which coincides with their findings for informal dimensions of social cohesion.

Other important findings in van der Meer and Tolsma's review concerned the effect of geography. The effects of ethnic diversity are stronger for neighborhoods and regions. The detrimental effects of ethnic diversity on intraneighborhood social cohesion appear to be universal or cross-cultural (van der Meer & Tolsma, 2014). However, there are broader contextual and perhaps sociocultural factors at play. Studies from the United States provide stronger support for constrict theory than do studies from other Western nations and societies (e.g., the United Kingdom, Canada, Australia), and the detrimental effects of ethnic diversity extend beyond intraneighborhood social cohesion to generalized trust in the United States. In sum, their review of the literature indicated that the effects of ethnic diversity were far from unequivocal and patterned by the specific aspects of ethnic diversity and social cohesion under investigation. In addition, the literature was characterized by several methodological problems and the absence of theory. With regard to methodological issues, for instance, several studies have not disentangled ethnic diversity from (relative) group sizes. Importantly, many studies lack rigor and use analytic approaches that do not capture the complex relationship(s) among diversity and social cohesion (e.g., bivariate statistics). Lastly, as argued here, but also pointed out by others (e.g., Putnam, 2007; van der Meer & Tolsma, 2014), there are different dimensions of diversity that have not been adequately assessed. The following are reviews of independent illustrative studies.

A study done in the United Kingdom illustrates the complex relationship between diversity and social capital as well as the limitations in the literature. Laurence (2011) investigated the association between neighborhood[12] ethnic diversity (using a similarity index[13]), disadvantage, and social capital (i.e., social trust, community involvement, and shared values) and intergroup relations (i.e., tolerance) at the individual level. The results indicated that increased neighborhood ethnic diversity was associated with less social capital, even when controlling for various individual- and community-level factors. Importantly, controlling for neighborhood disadvantage muted the negative effects of neighborhood ethnic diversity by about half. On the other hand, the effect of neighborhood diversity was positive for tolerance for diversity, controlling for neighborhood disadvantage, signaling that social capital and tolerance for diversity are distinct and independent constructs.[14] There was also some indication that the level of integration and ethnic neighborhood composition may be associated with differential levels of social capital and tolerance for diversity. Laurence also found a dampening effect of bridging ties on trust such that among those with more bridging ties, the negative effects of neighborhood diversity were less pronounced compared with those with social networks composed of bonding ties. This study provided support for the moderating and perhaps mediating role of bridging ties between diversity and social capital.

A study by Sampson and Graif (2009) highlights the positive role of diversity on social capital. Specifically, Sampson and Graif's (2009) study of Chicago neighborhoods showed that neighborhood ethnic diversity was not always associated with less social capital. Furthermore, the authors showed that immigrant status and racial diversity are positively related to

[12] Neighborhood was measured with an administrative areal unit, which consists of an average of 7200 residents.
[13] They used the Simpson Reciprocal Index of Diversity (Simpson, 1949), which is similar to the Herfindahl index reported previously.
[14] cf. bonding versus bridging social capital (Putnam, 2007).

specific dimensions of neighborhood social capital, undermining perhaps the chief theoretical underpinning of constrict theory (i.e., ethnic/racial homophily). Using multidimensional scaling (and clustering techniques), Sampson and Graif (2009) found four groups of neighborhoods based on their pairwise similarity on 15 residential social capital indicators. Communities with the lowest levels of diversity (and disadvantage) had the lowest levels of collective efficacy and resident organizational involvement.[15] Similarly, communities high on language and immigrant diversity had strong levels of conduct norms (though low levels of other dimensions of residential social capital), reflecting their strong family values, despite having medium levels of poverty, disadvantage, or residential stability (Sampson & Graif, 2009). In another community cluster (cosmopolitan efficacy), communities with high levels of neighborhood ethnic diversity also had high levels of collective efficacy and moderate levels of organizational involvement (but low levels of local networks or strong ties and conduct norms). Although these analyses reveal that different dimensions of diversity are positively associated with different dimensions of social capital, communities with low-to-moderate levels of diversity had the highest levels of social capital (save for conduct norms).

In descriptive analyses utilizing multiple datasets, researchers examined the effects of racial integration on intergroup relations among the four major ethnic/racial groups in the United States (Oliver, 2010; Oliver & Ha, 2008). Integrated neighborhoods were associated with both positive and negative intergroup relations. For instance, integrated neighborhoods are characterized by more interracial friendships as well as civic organization memberships—in short, bridging ties[16]—whereas segregated neighborhoods were characterized by fewer interracial friendships and ties. On the other hand, integrated neighborhoods are characterized by more social alienation and less social connectedness, particularly among European Americans. Furthermore, the effects of racial integration on intergroup relations varied by geography such that the effects of racial integration were positive at the local level (e.g., census tract) as opposed

[15] Yet even these communities were interested in and concerned with conserving their communities by seeking assistance from leaders.

[16] This finding came from the Social Capital Community Benchmark Survey (SCCBS). However, less integrated compared with more integrated neighborhoods were associated with more civic engagement (i.e., participation in voluntary organizations) and higher levels of social integration or cohesion (e.g., social trust, social belonging) among European Americans (Oliver & Ha, 2008).

to the regional level (e.g., metropolitan level; Oliver, 2010; Oliver & Ha, 2008). Despite its strengths and comprehensiveness, Oliver's and Oliver and Ha's research suffer from several issues. First, the analyses were mostly descriptive and do not fully capture the complexity and multidimensionality of social capital. As Laurence's (2011) study suggests, bridging ties (as well as other factors) may moderate and mediate the relationship between diversity and social capital.

Using representative data form the 2005 Citizenship Survey, Laurence and Heath (2008) performed a multilevel analysis of predictors of community social cohesion in England.[17] Their findings provide further insights into constrict theory and are largely consistent with a later study (Laurence, 2011). First, their findings do not support constrict theory—after controlling for other factors (e.g., age, gender, UK nativity, ethnicity, religion)—ethnic diversity was positively associated with community social cohesion. Furthermore, residential diversity was associated with higher levels of cohesion. On the other hand, immigration was negatively associated with social cohesion. Similarly, individual and area disadvantage, as well as perceived discrimination, was negatively associated with social cohesion, even after controlling for area ethnic diversity. Yet, not all disadvantaged neighborhoods were characterized by low levels of social cohesion. Importantly, social cohesion was increased by participation in formal voluntary associations, echoing Oliver and Ha's (2008) findings and conclusions on the beneficial effect of participation in civic associations on interracial relations in integrated neighborhoods.

In a case study of select communities, Maly (2005) intentionally focused on newly ethnically/racially integrated communities and how they managed the challenges facing integrated communities in the United States. These were Uptown, Chicago; Jackson Heights, NY; and San Antonio-Fruitvale, Oakland. These communities were ethnically/racially heterogeneous, though had no explicit aim to become so[18]—and had been diverse culturally and economically for several years (decades). A noteworthy feature of these communities is that they were able to combat larger social and institutional forces of racial separation (Maly, 2005). Specifically, and contrary to what constrict theory predicts, these communities engaged in

---

[17] *Community* was operationalized with an administrative areal unit, which consists of a minimum of 5000 and an average of 7200 residents.

[18] Maly distinguishes these unplanned diverse communities from "diverse-by-design" communities.

increased formal and behavioral forms of social capital on behalf of both minority and non-minority members of the community in response to numerous challenges. These communities were able to do so through a variety of means such as community redefinition and identity change. Although an insightful case study, an obvious limitation of this work concerns the selective nature of the sample, limited or questionable generalizability, and the qualitative nature of the findings. Despite the question of whether such positive responses to diversity can be replicated in other neighborhoods, Maly's work does show that diversity is not always or uniformly detrimental to interracial relations or social capital (cf. Wilson & Taub, 2006) and is important for at least three reasons: (a) it runs counter to constrict theory and certain social psychological perspectives (e.g., identity and threat perspectives), (b) it points out the many intentional challenges that integrated and integrating communities face (e.g., negative perceptions, views, and biases) in the United States, and (c) it expands our understanding of the ethnic homophily principle and extends this to other forms of homophily. These points are briefly discussed in the next section.

PERSPECTIVES ON DIVERSITY AND SOCIAL CAPITAL

Several explanations have been offered for constrict theory—the negative effects of ethnic diversity on social capital. The first are social psychological perspectives that focuses on social identity and group threat perspectives (Koopmans et al., 2015; van der Meer & Tolsma, 2014). Others focus on neighborhood as well as broader levels of socioeconomic inequality on social capital (e.g., Koopmans et al., 2015). Still others invoke ethnic homophily (van der Meer & Tolsma, 2014), and the rest focus on the role of cultural differences and associated resource management as well as coordination problems (Koopmans et al., 2015). Only a few of these explanations[19] (i.e., social psychological perspectives, broader social factors, and homophily) are briefly reviewed and discussed in order to provide the context for understanding how cultural perspectives might further contribute to our understanding of diversity and social capital.

---

[19] See Koopmans et al. (2015) for a thorough list of possible explanations, and van der Meer and Tolsma (2014) for a theoretical/conceptual model linking these various factors, which includes factors such as anomie, based on their review of the ethnic diversity and social cohesion literature.

Social Psychological Perspectives Social psychological perspectives invoked to support constrict theory emphasize social identity processes (e.g., categorization, in-group and out-group dynamics, in-group and out-group bias) and/or realistic conflict (e.g., Koopmans et al., 2015). They typically invoke well-established group phenomena involving a wide range of behaviors biased in favor of the in-group and against out-groups (e.g., Branscombe, Ellemers, Spears, & Doosje, 1999; Dovidio, Gaertner, & Esses, 2008; Tajfel & Turner, 1979). However, such behaviors occur under specific conditions (e.g., Branscombe et al., 1999; Ellemers & Haslam, 2012; Gaertner & Dovidio, 2012) and a stronger group identity is not necessarily associated with more in-group favoritism, out-group discrimination, or intergroup problems (Gaertner, Rust, Dovidio, Bachman, & Anastasio, 1996; Huo, Smith, Tyler, & Lind, 1996; Phinney, Jacoby, & Silva, 2007). In fact, there are many ways that individuals may emphasize, search for, or uphold a positive social identity (Ellemers & Haslam, 2012).

Although some studies have found support for social identity processes or realistic conflict (e.g., Alesina et al., 1999 found indirect support for the role of in-group favoritism; Alesina & Ferrara, 2000), neither can account for the positive effects of ethnic diversity on social capital and related outcomes (Koopmans et al., 2015). For instance, some researchers have not found significant associations between ethnic diversity and out-group attitudes among minorities—and have actually observed positive associations for Whites—in the United Kingdom (Schmid, Hewstone, & Al Ramiah, 2015). Similarly, other researchers have found that students at ethnically diverse schools hold more favorable out-group attitudes compared with those at less diverse schools (Hewstone et al., 2015). A field experimental study on cooperation conducted in Germany also failed to find support for in-group favoritism and/or out-group bias among Whites or ethnically diverse immigrants (Koopmans & Veit, 2014). Taken together, the equivocal effects of ethnic diversity on intergroup processes and relations may implicate the benefits of intergroup contact and erosion of interethnic boundaries (Koopmans et al., 2015)—which is supported by numerous social psychological studies and perspectives.

Just as an in-group identity can develop, and attendant biases and discriminatory behavior ensue (e.g., Tajfel, 1970), a more inclusive group identity can form wherein individuals, even those from different ethnic groups (Koopmans et al., 2015), identify with a superordinate group(s) (Dovidio et al., 2008). This process is described in the *Common In-group*

Identity Model (CIIM; Gaertner & Dovidio, 2000). The CIIM (Gaertner & Dovidio, 2000) is based on the *contact hypothesis*, which specifies that under certain conditions, more favorable intergroup attitudes and relations may emerge (Allport, 1954; Pettigrew & Tropp, 2006).[20] These conditions include common goals, status equality, and cooperation between groups as well as norms that encourage egalitarian intergroup relations (Gaertner & Dovidio, 2000).[21] Consistent with previously cited literature, economic inequality and disadvantage (e.g., Laurence, 2011; Laurence & Heath, 2008; Maly, 2005), as well as race-based inequality (e.g., racism), undermine intergroup relations and the formation of a common identity (Dovidio et al., 2008). Nevertheless, a common identity between minority and majority groups may be induced through cooperative interdependence as well as by emphasizing commonalities among members of different groups, even (Dovidio et al., 2008).

The benefits of a common identity include favorable intergroup attitudes, reduced bias and conflict, increased cooperation, helpful and other socially appropriate behavior, increased trust, resultant deeper relations (e.g., self-disclosing, forgiveness), as well as receptiveness to different perspectives and ideas (Dovidio et al., 2008). Importantly, a common identity does not necessitate the suppression of preexisting identities—even if the latter are strong. Rather, the CIIM allows for dual identities, much as bidimensional models of acculturation allow for the integration of two cultures (see the Subsection "Acculturation and Related Perspectives"; Dovidio et al., 2008; Dovidio, Gaertner, & Kafati, 2000), and this accommodation of identities may be beneficial for the self, in-group, and intergroup relations.

Area-Based Disadvantage and Inequality Neighborhood as well as broader levels of social and economic inequality may ultimately undermine social capital (e.g., social cohesion; Koopmans et al., 2015; Walton &

---

[20] Perhaps the most robust evidence for the contact hypothesis comes from a meta-analysis of 515 studies conducted in different countries and societies (Pettigrew & Tropp, 2006).

[21] See related sociological work that discusses similar processes and conditions on the development of panethnicity, which is on the rise in the United States (Okamoto & Mora, 2014). Panethnicity involves the maintenance of a specific in-group identity (Chinese American) and a superordinate identity (e.g., Asian American), and is achieved through a sense of cultural ties, solidarity, respect for diversity, and/or the need to address a common concern or issue (Okamoto & Mora, 2014), which at times is achieved through concerted efforts by leaders (cf. Maly, 2005; Walton & Hardebeck, 2016; Warren et al., 2001).

Hardebeck, 2016), and area-based ethnic diversity often coincides with economic disadvantage (Laurence, 2011; Nguyen, 2006; Sampson & Graif, 2009; van der Meer & Tolsma, 2014). Neighborhood disadvantage and other harmful neighborhood factors and conditions may thwart social capital through a variety of mechanisms such as increased powerlessness and mistrust, decreased interaction, as well as increased competition (Cheong et al., 2007; Laurence, 2011; Walton & Hardebeck, 2016). Thus, because ethnic minority groups are more likely to live in socioeconomically depressed neighborhoods (Nguyen, 2006; Sampson & Graif, 2009), ethnic diversity is confounded with neighborhood disadvantage (Alamilla et al., 2016; Maly, 2005; Roy, Hughes, & Yoshikawa, 2012), and its effects on social capital are obscured (Laurence, 2011). A related factor is ethnic residential segregation and/or ethnic density. Although segregation appears to be positively associated with in-group social connections, networks, and civic participation, it is negatively associated with bridging social capital and may be harmful to within-group identity (Oliver & Ha, 2008; Oyserman & Yoon, 2009). In general, discrimination and negative contexts of reception for new immigrants discourage social capital, even among more established immigrant groups (Cheong et al., 2007).

Homophily Although some scholarship supports the positive relationship between ethnic homophily and certain forms of social capital (McPherson et al., 2001; Neat & Watling Neal, 2014; see the 2017 special section on "diversity and sense of community" in the *American Journal of Community Psychology*), other research suggests the importance of other forms of homophily to social capital. For instance, although the United States remains highly ethnically segregated residentially (Johnston, Poulsen, & Forrest, 2007; Maly, 2005; Massey & Denton, 1993; Oliver, 2010; Oliver & Ha, 2008; van der Meer & Tolsma, 2014), data indicates that ethnic residential segregation declined in the last three decades of the twentieth century (Maly, 2005; Massey, Rothwell, & Domina, 2009), and that integrated neighborhoods are becoming more widespread and stable (Maly, 2005). During this same period socioeconomic segregation has increased and has been accompanied by a concomitant decline in overt ethnic prejudice and possibly ethnic homophily (Massey et al., 2009). These trends have been accompanied by segregation along sociopolitical ideological lines during the first years of the twenty-first century (Massey et al., 2009), signaling the importance of other types of homophily, such as value homophily or similarity in attitudes, beliefs, and values (cf. horizontal dimension of individualism and collectivism; Lazarsfeld & Merton, 1954; McPherson et al., 2001).

CULTURAL PERSPECTIVES ON DIVERSITY AND SOCIAL CAPITAL

Cultural differences and associated resource management, as well as coordination problems, may help explain some of the equivocal findings for constrict theory (Koopmans et al., 2015). However, this possible mechanism has been understudied and undertheorized in the extant literature. From a cross-cultural psychological perspective, cultural similarity (dissimilarity) is a critical factor in intercultural relations as well as in individual and group adaptation (e.g., Berry, Kim, Power, Young, & Bujaki, 1989; Berry, 2006a). Possible mechanisms for these intergroup processes are illuminated with cultural and cross-cultural psychological perspectives.

Cross-cultural psychologists have identified cultural factors or dimensions that differentiate societies. These dimensions represent solutions to external adaptation (i.e., survival) as well as internal integration (i.e., "how to stay together"), and consist of both values and practices (Schein, 1992 as cited in Javidan & Hauser, 2004, p. 103). In an ambitious cross-cultural study in 62 societies[22] (House, Hanges, Javida, Dofrman, & Gupta, 2004), researchers reliably identified the following cultural dimensions: uncertainty avoidance (degree to which uncertainty is avoided through various behavioral means), power distance (degree to which power should be concentrated or distributed), individualism and collectivism (I-C), gender egalitarianism, assertiveness (degree to which confrontation and aggression are normalized in social relationships), future orientation (cf. uncertainty avoidance), performance orientation (degree to which performance is valued and rewarded), and humane orientation (degree to which altruism, kindness, fairness, etc. are valued and rewarded; House & Javidan, 2004), which have been corroborated by different research programs over time (Fischer, 2014; Hofstede, 1980; Schwartz, 1992, 1994). Other critical dimensions between societies exist, such as the strength of cultural

---

[22] The Global Leadership and Organizational Behavior Effectiveness (GLOBE) Research Program.

norms and tolerance of individual deviation from them (*tightness* versus *looseness*; Gelfand et al., 2011).

Not only are several of these dimensions important at the individual, organizational, and societal levels, but they may also play a role in the development or maintenance of social capital among groups. For instance, collectivist groups are characterized by interconnectedness, interdependence, and relatedness, whereas individualistic groups are characterized by autonomy, independence, and rationality (Gelfand et al., 2004; Kitayama et al., 2007). *High-performance orientation* cultures value control over the environment, whereas cultures low on this dimension value harmony with the environment (Javidan, 2004). Societies that score lower on *assertiveness* value modesty, persons and relationships, cooperation, equality, and solidarity as opposed to societies higher on it, which value dominance, competition, and instrumentality as opposed to relationality (Den Hartog, 2004). Similarly, societies with higher levels of *humane orientation* are characterized by friendliness, tolerance for mistakes, altruism, benevolence, kindness, generosity, concern for others (including strangers), strength of relationships, concern for ethnic discrimination, high social support, and familism (Kabasakal & Bodur, 2004).

Clearly, these cultural dimensions—and some in particular—are interrelated (e.g., humane orientation and I-C; Kabasakal & Bodur, 2004) and have potential implications for social capital and intergroup relations in diverse communities. In fact, experimental evidence indicates that values' similarity between nations may mitigate realistic (e.g., economic, power asymmetry) threats as well as enhance intergroup attitudes and relations (Garcia-Retamero, Müller, & Rousseau, 2012). Consistent with empirical clustering of societies (Gupta & Hanges, 2004), cultural (religious) differences between ethnocultural and national youth were associated with a preference for acculturation strategy. For instance, Muslim youth endorsed a national orientation the least (Phinney, Berry, Vedder, & Liebkind, 2006).

Although groups may possess unique cultural values and dimensions (e.g., Fischer, 2014), there is convergence and overlap among them. For instance, among African American, Asian American, and Latino/a American populations, values are placed on collectivism, communalism, familism, family obligation, and spirituality (Kim & Abreu, 2001; Kim, Li, & Ng, 2005; Kim, Soliz, Orellana, & Alamilla, 2009; Obasi & Leong, 2010; Schwartz et al., 2010). Cultural values of communalism, familism, and filial piety, although associated with different ethnic groups and regions of the world, are interrelated and accounted for by the same underlying collectivist-based cultural value (Schwartz et al., 2010). Importantly, individuals with diverging values, dimensions, and worldviews can coexist and cooperate with one another (Phinney et al., 2006; Prodi, 2004). In the interest of space, and because cultural dimensions are conceptually interrelated and several appear to be related to I-C, this cultural dimension and its implications for social capital and intergroup relations are discussed further.[23]

Individualism and Collectivism (I-C) Central to I-C are the concepts of independence and interdependence, respectively (Kitayama et al., 2007; Markus & Kitayama, 1991). Key features of individualism and independence are defining oneself as an autonomous and independent being, prioritizing personal goals over group goals, and an internal frame of reference, whereas those of collectivism and interdependence are defining oneself in terms of key groups, prioritizing group goals over individual goals, and a focus on context in decision-making processes (Kitayama et al., 2007; Markus & Kitayama, 1991).

I-C are multifaceted and multidimensional. For one, there is a distinction between I-C values versus practices (Gelfand et al., 2004). Second, I-C may operate differently depending on the level of analysis (Gelfand et al., 2004). Third, Triandis (1994, 1995) identified at least two types or additional dimensions of I-C: *vertical* and *horizontal*. Whereas the former stresses hierarchy and unequal-status relationships, the latter stresses egalitarian and equal-status relationships (Gelfand et al., 2004). Societies and groups may be characterized by vertical or horizontal social relationships and individualism or collectivism.

Individuals may possess aspects of I-C (i.e., idiocentrism and allocentrism; Allik & Realo, 2004; Gelfand et al., 2004; Oyserman, Coon, & Kemmelmeier, 2002; Triandis, Leung, Villareal, & Clark, 1985). In their review of studies on I-C, Triandis and Gelfand (2012) pointed out that collectivistic (or individualistic) behavior could be primed with collectivistic (or individualistic) themes. One implication of this is that groups char-

---

[23] Furthermore, I-C has a long history in human societies as well as in cultural psychology, and has been shown to be related to a host of individual, group, and societal phenomena (Gelfand et al., 2004; Kitayama et al., 2007; Markus & Kitayama, 1991; Oyserman, Coon, & Kemmelmeier, 2002; Triandis & Gelfand, 2012). However, other cultural dimensions are theoretically relevant and important.

acterized by higher levels of collectivism may prime collectivistic behavior (cf. Alamilla et al., 2016). Another is that individuals who may belong to either a primarily individualistic or a collectivistic group may engage in different behaviors under specific conditions (Oyserman et al., 2002).

I-C and Its Implications for Social Capital Collectivism has been associated with increased relationality and other behaviors associated with a more communal orientation and lifestyle, such as less of a concern on time and a stronger concern for the well-being of others, stronger tendency to engage in group activities, greater cooperation, greater organizational citizenship, less confrontational conflict resolution styles, importance of extended family networks, and lower relationship dissolution rates (Gelfand et al., 2004; Oyserman et al., 2002; Triandis & Gelfand, 2012). Strong support for the association between collectivism and relationality comes from a meta-analysis by Oyserman et al. (2002) with diverse samples. Among the many interesting and counterintuitive findings, collectivism was associated with higher levels of obligation to individuals as well as society among different ethnic groups. Similarly, Gelfand et al. (2004) also found significant positive associations between in-group collectivistic practices and values with strength of family ties as well as between practices and respect for family and friends at the societal level.

Individualism has been associated with several processes antithetical to a communal orientation and lifestyle (Allik & Realo, 2004; Gelfand et al., 2004),[24] such as a rapid pace of life, strong focus on individual achievement, individual mobility, less organizational cooperation, greater sense of alienation and loneliness, more confrontational conflict resolution styles, and higher relationship dissolution rates (Gelfand et al., 2004; Triandis & Gelfand, 2012; Osyerman et al., 2002; Triandis et al., 1985). Yet studies have demonstrated that individualism is associated with increased rather than decreased social capital. Analyzing relationships for 48 American states and 37 nations and controlling for economic factors at the state or national level, Allik and Realo (2004) found that institutional individualism was positively associated with social capital and institutional collectivism was negatively associated with social capital among American states and other nations (Allik & Realo, 2004). At the national level, institutional

---

[24] These, in turn, have been argued to undermine individual and societal well-being as well as social capital.

individualism was positively associated with interpersonal trust and civic engagement, yet the association became non-significant for interpersonal trust after controlling for economic factors (e.g., gross domestic product [GDP]). Two important exceptions were noted: the US state of Utah and the country of China, both of which had high levels of collectivism and social capital.

These results were largely supported in a follow-up study examining in-group and institutional dimensions of collectivism on social capital (i.e., interpersonal trust, participation in voluntary associations) in 45 countries (Realo, Allik, & Greenfield, 2008). Of particular import was the negative correlation between in-group collectivism and interpersonal trust, but positive correlation for institutional collectivism and interpersonal trust. These correlations persisted after accounting for GDP per capita. Results from multiple regression analyses revealed that in-group collectivism was negatively associated with both dimensions of social capital, whereas institutional collectivism was positively associated with interpersonal trust (but not voluntary associations), even after controlling for GDP per capita. Lastly, in-group collectivism was negatively associated with participation in most types of voluntary associations (10 out of 15), whereas institutional collectivism was positively associated with two types of voluntary associations (labor unions and church or religious organizations), even after controlling for GDP per capita. The authors did not examine any dimensions of individualism in their study, nor were other, more proximal covariates included in any of these analyses.

A study on the associations between different dimensions of I-C and social capital at the individual level[25] among Estonians revealed different patterns (Beilmann & Realo, 2012). Using data from the Estonian Survey of Culture and Personality, the authors found that only one dimension of individualism (mature self-responsibility) was positively associated with social capital; the other two individualism dimensions were negatively associated with social capital. All three dimensions of collectivism were positively associated with social capital (however, the familism dimension was statistically not significant). These findings were generally preserved even when controlling for age and education. Although interesting, these findings were only correlational in nature.

---

[25] Social capital has been argued to be and often treated as a property of the collective rather than of individuals (e.g., Putnam, 2000).

Although important, these studies (e.g., Allik & Realo, 2004; Beilmann & Realo, 2012) have several limitations. First, they are correlational and do not tell us how I-C and social capital are impacted by other variables. The findings also likely misrepresent the association between I-C and social capital because of possible equivalence issues (van de Vijver & Matsumoto, 2012) and because I-C as well as social capital may differ across cultures or groups (Beilmann & Realo, 2012; Gelfand et al., 2004; Oyserman et al., 2002; Triandis & Gelfand, 2012). Furthermore, I-C is multidimensional and dimensionality matters (Gelfand et al., 2004; Realo et al., 2008; Triandis & Gelfand, 2012). Importantly, the findings do not inform us of the interaction of diversity, I-C, and social capital among groups at different geographical levels of analysis. Scholars have observed that the effects of diversity on social capital (e.g., social cohesion, intergroup relations) vary depending on the level of geographical analysis (Oliver, 2010; Oliver & Ha, 2008; Putnam, 2007; van der Meer & Tolsma, 2014). Thus, it is possible that the relationship between I-C and social capital is moderated by contextual factors (e.g., Allik & Realo, 2004), such as the extent to which the environment supports I-C (cf. Alamilla et al., 2016; Oyserman et al., 2002). There are broader factors that may impact social capital (Cheong et al., 2007; Laurence, 2011; Laurence & Heath, 2008), such as labor unions, the welfare state, and societal differences in subjective well-being as well as other indicators of national well-being (Radcliff, 2008; Tov & Diener, 2008). Lastly, more work is needed on the relationship between other cultural dimensions and social capital.

Acculturation, Assimilation, and Integration/Inclusion Societies differ with respect to attitudes and policies toward immigration as well as toward ethnocultural diversity, ranging from welcoming to hostile (Berry, 2006a; Berry, Westin, Virta, Vedder, Rooney, & Sang, 2006). Societies may endorse *multiculturalism*, which is characterized by the widespread value of cultural diversity, relatively low levels of societal prejudice, ethnocentrism and ethnic discrimination, positive mutual attitudes among ethnocultural groups, and a sense of attachment to and identification with the larger society by all individuals and groups. Many societies have endorsed the *melting pot* metaphor or *assimilation*,[26] requiring immigrants and minorities to blend into mainstream culture and society, although they

---

[26] When this policy is strongly enforced, it is more like a "pressure cooker" (Berry, 2006a).

may be allowed to privately espouse their heritage culture (van Oudenhoven, 2006). Some societies have elected *segregation*, which refers to the forced separation of immigrant or minority groups from the larger society, and others *exclusion* (also called ethnocide; Berry, 2003), which refers to the marginalization of immigrant or minority groups by the dominant group or larger society.

Following intercultural contact, individuals undergo an adjustment or adaptation process known as acculturation (e.g., Berry, Phinney, Sam, & Vedder, 2006). This process consists of psychological (e.g., psychological well-being) as well as sociocultural (e.g., acquisition of skills and behaviors required in the new society) adaptation (Berry, Phinney, et al., 2006). Acculturation entails changes in a variety of domains, including behaviors, knowledge, identity, and values (e.g., I-C), as a result of being in contact with other cultures (Alamilla et al., 2016; Kim & Abreu, 2001; Kim & Alamilla, 2017). However, individuals may also undergo (re)learning or (re)socialization of their heritage culture (Kim & Alamilla, 2017), a process known as enculturation. For non-Westerners, acculturation typically involves adopting aspects of individualism in part or in whole, whereas enculturation involves retaining (or reacquiring) aspects of collectivism in part or in whole (cf. Alamilla et al., 2016).

Although the importance of contextual factors to the acculturation process for individuals was acknowledged by early scholars (Redfield, Linton, & Herskovits, 1936; Berry, 1974), only recently have these factors received attention from researchers (Alamilla et al., 2016; Birman & Simon, 2014; Kim & Alamilla, 2017). Often missing from this literature are the broader social and contextual factors that thwart or facilitate the acculturation process and related outcomes. For instance, individuals may adopt one of several acculturation strategies during intercultural contact (Berry, 1974, 1980)—which parallel those occurring at the societal level. For instance, an individual may pursue an *integration strategy*, which refers to the individual's maintenance of the heritage culture as well as participation in other cultures. On the other hand, an individual may pursue *assimilation*, which refers to the individual's abandonment of the heritage culture in favor of participation in other cultures. However, a given society may not afford certain individuals with all acculturation options (Berry, 1974) or may be characterized by a lack of a multicultural orientation, high rates of prejudice, racism, and discrimination, which may result in a weak attachment to the host society (Berry, 2003). Thus, adopting a separation or marginalization strategy may be the result of an individual's failed attempts at assimilation because of discrimination from the host society (Berry, 2003). In fact, in a large-scale study of youth in 13 societies, the separation strategy (i.e., stronger involvement with the heritage culture relative to the host culture) was the second-most preferred strategy among ethnocultural youth, whereas assimilation was among national youth (Phinney ct al., 2006).

From an intergroup perspective, the integration strategy appears to be especially beneficial for social capital, as integrated individuals are connected to their in-group as well as to the host culture (Dovidio et al., 2000, 2008; Oliver & Ha, 2008). As such, they are likely to feel connected to and take interest in their ethnocultural communities (Oliver & Ha, 2008) as well as have more interracial ties (Oliver, 2010). Conversely, marginalized individuals may be alienated from their ethnocultural communities and not take an active interest in civic organizations (Oliver & Ha, 2008). Large-scale research suggests that ethnocultural and national youth both highly endorse integration over assimilation acculturation strategies (Phinney et al., 2006). There are personal benefits to an integrated or bicultural approach as well, which may have implications for enhanced intergroup relations (Dovidio et al., 2000, 2008; Kim & Omizo, 2005, 2006, 2010).

Although some societies claim they embrace multiculturalism, evidence suggests otherwise. In a large-scale study, although over one-third of ethnocultural youth reported a high degree of involvement with their heritage and host cultures (e.g., speaking both languages, endorsing heritage cultural values, interacting with the in-group and national group), national youth preferred higher levels of acculturation (assimilation) (Phinney et al., 2006). In contrast to earlier waves of immigrants to the United States (mostly Europeans), recent waves of immigrants face serious challenges to societal integration such as widespread societal racism and racialization, exclusion, marginalization, and blocked opportunity (Alamilla et al., 2016; Nguyen, 2006; Portes & Rumbaut, 2001; Telles & Ortiz, 2008). Similar challenges confront immigrants in Europe. For instance, since 2008, non-European Union (EU) citizens raced a 4% increase in their risk of poverty or social exclusion—a rate double that of EU citizens (Migration Integration Policy Index, MIPEX, 2015). Although contact and competition/threat may represent different stages of the same process (e.g., Laurence & Heath, 2008), which is only likely to increase with globalization, broader social factors such as community deprivation, inequality, hostile immigration, and diversity policies will undermine and thwart the acculturation, assimilation, and integration process (Berry, Westin et al., 2006; Cheong et al., 2007; Juang & Cookston, 2009; Laurence & Heath, 2008; Maly, 2005; Nguyen, 2006; Portes & Rumbaut, 2001; Telles & Ortiz, 2008; van der Meer & Tolsma, 2014).[27]

DISCUSSION

The present chapter focused on providing a deeper understanding of the relationship between diversity and social capital as well as intergroup relations in the United States. A major goal of the current chapter was to disentangle ethnicity, cultural factors, and related broader factors (e.g., neighborhood disadvantage). The central question explored is, what possible role do cultural factors have in the relationship between different measures of diversity and social capital among groups?

Despite strong claims by some, diversity—including ethnic diversity—is not equivocally associated with decreased social capital (Koopmans et al., 2015; van der Meer & Tolsma, 2014). The relationship is complex and depends on a number of factors that have not been adequately addressed in research. These include geography or context, dimension of diversity (e.g., immigration vs. ethnic diversity), dimension of social capital, proportion of ethnic persons in a community, and presence of bridging ties in a community (Lancee & Schaeffer, 2015; Laurence & Heath, 2008; Oliver & Ha, 2008; Putnam, 2007; van der Meer & Tolsma, 2014). Importantly, many studies have confounded neighborhood ethnic diversity with neighborhood disadvantage (e.g., Alamilla et al., 2016; Roy et al., 2012), the latter of which has been shown to diminish social capital and social bonding (Cheong et al., 2007; Laurence, 2011; Laurence & Heath, 2008; Putnam, 2001; van der Meer & Tolsma, 2014).

A more significant omission from the broader social capital literature is the role of broader social factors, including issues of social justice (Putnam, 2001) and inequality. For instance, global economic inequality is linked with local economic inequality as well as with migration: "One should see migration as a part of globalization and global inequality. In other words, it's not an issue that just fell off from the sky; it's an issue that is actually very much present in the structure of [global] inequality that we have"

---

[27] It is important to note that lower human capital associated with certain immigrant groups may also impact societal attitudes toward these groups (Koopmans, 2013).

(B. Milanovic, personal communication, May 9, 2016).[28] Currently, the United States and Europe are experiencing a rise in nationalism, nativism, and anti-immigrant sentiment, ostensibly because of a rise in immigration in these countries (Amnesty International, 2017; Cheong et al., 2007; Human Rights Watch, 2017).[29] Regardless of causality, policies floated by and rhetoric from government and other influential leaders may fuel anti-immigrant sentiment as well as negative reactions to ethnocultural diversity (Berry, Westin, et al., 2006; Callens, 2015; Cheong et al., 2007), resulting in racial division and segregation (Maly, 2005; Oliver, 2010), individual adaptation problems (Berry, Phinney, et al., 2006), as well as the perceived erosion of social capital (Cheong et al., 2007; Koopmans et al., 2015). A considerable amount of research highlights the toxic effects of racism, bias, and so on and their thwarting effects on the integration of diverse individuals into their respective societies (Juang & Cookston, 2009; Nguyen, 2006; Portes & Rumbaut, 2001; Phinney et al., 2006; Telles & Ortiz, 2008). Ethnically diverse individuals may cope with such rejection through a process of devaluing the dimension that is a source of their stress as well as withdrawal (Thoits, 2010, 2013), leading to a devaluating of integration and assimilation, and withdrawal from the larger society and civic life (Juang & Cookston, 2009; Nguyen, 2006; Portes & Rumbaut, 2001; Phinney et al., 2006; Telles & Ortiz, 2008). An important point is that what appears to be problems resulting from ethnic diversity may really be the result of broader factors (Landis & Albert, 2012), and that policies and influential shapers of public opinion can exacerbate or attenuate anti-multiculturalism as well as perceptions of diversity as a threat to social capital (Cheong et al., 2007). Without policies on pro-diversity, pro-integration, and so on, ethnically diverse as well integrated communities will continue to face serious challenges (e.g., Maly, 2005; Smith, 1993) and diversity will be seen as a threat to social capital.

---

[28] Refer to the Elephant Chart in Milanovic (2016) for data linking global inequality with migration and the rise of nationalism in developed countries, for instance.

[29] See, for instance, an online discussion on a White nationalist website (https://www.stormfront.org/forum/t120656-2/), wherein members admonish one another to avoid "bad arguments" such as conflating *immigrants* with *immigration*, adding that it is the latter not the former that is "harmful to our society."

NEED FOR CULTURAL PERSPECTIVES

Cultural perspectives are needed in light of relevant limitations of focusing on ethnic diversity. Importantly, because diversity may lead to increased anomie and the undermining of values, behavior, and norms conducive to social capital and social cohesion (Koopmans et al., 2015; Oliver & Ha, 2008; van der Meer & Tolsma, 2014), a new focus should be on values, behavior, and norms. Furthermore, because social capital is tied to the societal values, norms, and practices of the dominant group (at the expense of "foreigners"; Cheong et al., 2007),[30] cultural perspectives may illuminate cases in which the former are compatible and incompatible for the development of social capital and positive intergroup relations. As illustrated in this chapter, many ethnic minorities and immigrants may have values and norms that are different from those of the receiving society. As such, any observed negative effects on social capital because of diversity among newly integrating communities may be the result of cultural dissimilarity, issues of ethnocultural bias aside (Cheong et al., 2007; Oliver, 2010).

As noted previously, perceptions of cultural similarity may facilitate intergroup contact and relations (e.g., Gaertner & Dovidio, 2000). According to the CIIM (Gaertner & Dovidio, 2000), perceptions of cultural similarity may positively affect social capital and intergroup relations through recategorization and development of a superordinate common identity (i.e., humanistic, collectivistic), reducing cognitive, affective, and motivational sources of bias (Gaertner & Dovidio, 2012). Recategorization and a common identity may (a) lead to an expanded self-concept (cf. Kitayama et al., 2007; Markus & Kitayama, 1991), (b) increase perceptions of similarity within groups (e.g., perceptions of shared factors), (c) reduce identity threat, (d) increase perspective-taking, (e) increase favorable attributions of behavior, and (f) increase compassion, empathy, and so on (Gaertner & Dovidio, 2012). In diverse communities, perceptions of cultural similarity may lead to perceived alignment in worldviews, which may minimize a sense of isolation and increase one's sense of social cohesion and integration (cf. Alamilla et al., 2016), as well as self-efficacy (Saegert & Carpiano, 2017).

Such communities may experience increased contact, meaningful social interaction, enhanced intergroup relations, and stronger community ties

---

[30] For this reason, social capital must be clearly and critically defined as well as disentangled from cultural differences, societal biases, and prejudices.

(Alamilla et al., 2016). Additionally, such communities may afford individuals with beneficial social networks as well as a social environment and climate that are sensitive to cultural maintenance. At minimum, respect and reciprocity (e.g., interpersonal harmony) may ensue and result in positive intergroup relations and increased social capital. Although strong ties (i.e., boding social capital) are not necessary for other forms of social capital or collective self-efficacy (Raudenbush & Sampson, 1999; Sampson, 2001; Sampson, Raudenbush, & Earls, 1997), cultural factors may facilitate acting on behalf of community values and norms (Sampson & Graif, 2009).

Important Considerations Cultural factors may pose certain real challenges. For one, members of different ethnocultural groups may experience discomfort, anxiety, and perhaps stress because of intercultural contact (Organista, Marin, & Chun, 2010). Individuals may realize that their cultural norms, beliefs, values, and so on are one among many (Organista et al., 2010).[31] Yet intercultural contact can be beneficial for a number of reasons, as previously noted. For one, some individuals may come to recognize the underlying similarities among their cultures: with as many as 80% of the world's population considered collectivistic (Heine, 2012), many ethnic groups may share similar underlying cultural patterns (as opposed to surface and obvious cultural differences; cf. Kim & Abreu, 2001; Zea, Asner-Self, Birman, & Buki, 2003). Furthermore, intercultural contact is typically conducive to (if not necessary for) decreased prejudice and discrimination (Allport, 1954; Dovidio et al., 2008; Gaertner & Dovidio, 2000; Maly, 2005; Pettigrew & Tropp, 2006). Another issue challenge concerns collectivism and group identities. A large body of social psychological research has indicated that a stronger identification with one's primary group is characteristic of collectivist cultures (Gelfand et al., 2004; Triandis & Gelfand, 2012), and strong group identities *may* have implications for intergroup relations such as identity threat, in-group bias, and discrimination against out-groups (e.g., Branscombe et al., 1999; Oyserman et al., 2002).[32] Yet a stronger social

---

[31] These difficulties can be exacerbated by hostile or negative societal integration attitudes and policies (e.g., Cheong et al., 2007; Koopmans et al., 2015; Maly, 2005; Nguyen, 2006; van der Meer & Tolsma, 2014).

[32] This may be more an issue upon initial contact and with immigrant populations that have not developed a dual identity (e.g., Brazilian versus Brazilian American).

identity[33] need not always lead to in-group preference, out-group bias, discrimination, or competition (Ellemers & Haslam, 2012; Phinney et al., 2007).

RECOMMENDATIONS FOR FUTURE RESEARCH

Based on the review of the literature, several recommendations seem warranted. Researchers should first explore the antecedents and consequences of bonding social capital among groups in diverse communities. Such studies should take place in the context of broader scholarship on multiculturalism and cultural pluralism in diverse societies. Researchers should address different dimensions of diversity (e.g., ethnicity, immigrant status) *as well as* cultural factors. To the extent possible, researchers should assess the role of cultural factors (e.g., uncertainty avoidance, power distance, I-C, assertiveness, future orientation, humane orientation; House & Javidan, 2004). Compatibility with regard to these dimensions may have main effects, as well as moderating and/or mediating effects, on select dimensions of social capital as well as on intergroup processes.[34] Studies should assess whether and how sociocultural factors as well as different forms of diversity positively and negatively affect communities, net of other factors. Such research should distinguish between actual and perceptions of cultural similarity (cf. Pettigrew et al., 2010; Wagner, Christ, Pettigrew, Stellmacher, & Wolf, 2006). Other identities and statuses as well as their interactions should also be assessed (e.g., Neal & Watling Neal, 2014).

Because research has revealed that not all dimensions of social capital are uniformly influenced by diversity, researchers should assess different dimensions of social capital. Furthermore, because it is possible that social capital functions as an intervening variable (e.g., Oliver & Ha, 2008), future studies should model social capital non-recursively or in a feedback loop. In addition to social capital outcomes such as bridging social capital, social support, cultural humility, racial tolerance, interracial respect and trust, as well as integration should be examined, as these may be more appropriate for diverse and plural societies such as the United States (Kim & Alamilla, 2017; Laurence, 2011; Neal & Watling Neal, 2014; Oliver & Ha, 2008; Saegert & Carpiano, 2017; Townley et al., 2011). Related

---

[33] Nor do these constitute the only identity management strategies (Ellemers & Haslam, 2012).

[34] However, see Maly (2005) on the intentional role of outside forces in a community's ethnic composition and thus intergroup relations.

concepts such as collective efficacy should also be examined. Collective efficacy refers to the degree of social cohesion along with the capacity/ ability to intervene or act on behalf of community values and norms (Sampson, 2001; Sampson, Raudenbush, & Earls, 1997; Warren et al., 2001), and has been shown to be compatible with diversity (Sampson & Graif, 2009). Clearly, cultural dimensions, values, and worldviews appear relevant to collective efficacy.

Future studies should adequately assess different geographical as well as spatial dimensions of diversity, culture, and social capital, as these appear to be context dependent (Allik & Realo, 2004; Beilmann & Realo, 2012; Oliver & Ha, 2008; Realo et al., 2008; Sampson & Graif, 2009; van der Meer & Tolsma, 2014). Culture has different conceptual and empirical implications at the individual and higher levels (Alamilla et al., 2016; Gelfand et al., 2004; Hanges & Dickson, 2004; Hanges, Dickson, & Sipe, 2004; House & Hanges, 2004). Thus, research should simultaneously include smaller levels of analysis as well as larger ones for diversity, culture, and social capital. Lastly, spatial autocorrelation, the association or dependence between measurements of the same variable taken at two distinct locations as a function of spatial proximity (Anselin, 1988), is present for diversity and social capital, and this requires special spatial–analytic considerations (Sampson & Graif, 2009). Thus, special methods are needed for assessing the complex ways that diversity and social capital are related across places and space (Pierce, 2010; Sampson & Graif, 2009; Sampson, Morenoff, & Gannon-Rowley, 2002).

Given the importance of the broader contextual factors to social capital, such as socioeconomic factors, segregation, sociocultural–historical factors, official policies, and public opinion-shapers (Allik & Realo, 2004; Berry, Phinney, et al., 2006; Cheong et al., 2007; Laurence, 2011; Laurence & Heath, 2008; Maly, 2005; van der Meer & Tolsma, 2014; Warren et al., 2001), future studies should appropriately address these, perhaps using mixed methods. To the extent that the immediate, surrounding, and larger social context is hostile to diversity, differences, and so on, and not measured, studies on the effects of diversity may yield mixed or contradictory findings. This is perhaps true for studies that address cultural factors, but fail to address broader contextual factors. More proximal factors associated with certain dimensions of social capital such as community economic deprivation and socioeconomic factors[35] (Koopmans et al.,

---

[35] For civic engagement/participation, individual interest and catalysts for such participation are more proximal (Verba, Schlozman, & Brady, 1995 as cited in Oliver & Ha, 2008).

2015; Laurence, 2011; Laurence & Heath, 2008; Maly, 2005; van der Meer & Tolsma, 2014) should be included in models.

The degree of residential ethnic as well as economic segregation deserves critical attention (van der Meer & Tolsma, 2014). Studies examining the direct effects of ethnic density on aspects of social capital are rare (van der Meer & Tolsma, 2014). Future research should include individual as well as different area-based measures of disadvantage, but also model the individual as well as contextual effects associated with the differential human capital of groups (e.g., Koopmans, 2013). Scholars have observed that it is disadvantage that likely plays a confounding role in the relationship between ethnic diversity and social capital (Laurence, 2011; Laurence & Heath, 2008; van der Meer & Tolsma, 2014). Specifically, they argue that diversity, residential segregation, and inequality synergistically undermine social cohesion and should thus be jointly addressed (at least by policy-makers).

CONCLUSIONS

Diversity is not unequivocally or uniformly associated with diminished social capital. The notion (and scholarship) that diversity is fundamentally incompatible with social capital ignores the undermining role of larger contextual factors and social forces such as racism, xenophobia, anti-immigrant sentiment, and hostile policies toward ethnocultural groups (Berry, Westin, et al., 2006; Bonilla-Silva, 2000; Cheong et al., 2007; Dovidio et al., 2008; Juang & Cookston, 2009; Laurence & Heath, 2008; Maly, 2005; Nguyen, 2006; Oliver & Ha, 2008; van der Meer & Tolsma, 2014).

Despite its powerful capacity for division, race and racial separation (i.e., segregation) are not natural but rather socially constructed (Maly, 2005; Oliver, 2010; Zinn, 2003). Racial hostility (e.g., segregation) and its concomitant ills are actively shaped, encouraged, and maintained (Maly, 2005). As noted by US historian Howard Zinn (2003):

> Black and White worked together, fraternized together. The very fact that laws had to be passed after a while to forbid such relations indicates the strength of that tendency. In 1661 a law was passed in Virginia that "in case any English servant shall run away in company of any Negroes" he would have to give special service for extra years to the master of the runaway Negro. In 1691, Virginia provided for the banishment of any "white man or woman being free who shall intermarry with a negro, mulatoo, or Indian

man or woman bond or free." ... The point is that the elements of this web are historical, not "natural." ... It means only that there is a possibility for something else, under historical conditions not yet realized. (pp. 31–38)

Understanding and addressing cultural differences and similarities might help in moving toward a different a set of conditions for improved intergroup relations (House, 2004) and more inclusive forms of community (Krause & Montenegro, 2017).

REFERENCES

Alamilla, S. G., Scott, M. A., & Hughes, D. L. (2016). The relationship of individual-level and community-level sociocultural and neighbourhood factors to the mental health of ethnic groups in two large U.S. cities. *Journal of Community Psychology, 44*(1), 51–77. https://doi.org/10.1002/jcop.21742.

Albert, R. D., Gabrielsen, S., & Landis, D. (2012). Ethnic conflict from an interdisciplinary perspective: Lessons learned, policy implications, and recommendations for conflict amelioration and peace building. In D. Landis, R. D. Albert, D. Landis, & R. D. Albert (Eds.), *Handbook of ethnic conflict: International perspectives* (pp. 587–630). New York, NY: Springer. https://doi.org/10.1007/978-1-4614-0448-4_22.

Alesina, A., Baqir, R., & Easterly, W. (1999). Public goods and ethnic divisions. *Quarterly Journal of Economics, 114*(4), 1243–1284.

Alesina, A., & Ferrara, E. L. (2000). Participation in heterogeneous communities. *Quarterly Journal of Economics, 115*(3), 847–904. https://doi.org/10.1162/003355300554935.

Allik, J., & Realo, A. (2004). Individualism-collectivism and social capital. *Journal of Cross-Cultural Psychology, 35*(1), 29–49. https://doi.org/10.1177/0022022103260381.

Allport, G. W. (1954). *The nature of prejudice.* Reading, MA: Addison Wesley.

Amnesty International. (2017). *Amnesty International Report 2016/17: The state of the world's human rights.* London, UK: Peter Benenson House. Retrieved from https://www.amnesty.org/en/documents/pol10/4800/2017/en/

Anselin, L. (1988). *Spatial econometrics: Methods and models.* Dordrecht, Netherlands: Kluwer Academic.

Beilmann, M., & Realo, A. (2012). Individualism-collectivism and social capital at the individual level. *TRAMES: A Journal of the Humanities & Social Sciences, 16*(3), 205–217. https://doi.org/10.3176/tr.2012.3.01.

Berry, J. W. (1974). An ecological approach to cross cultural psychology. *Man-Environment Systems, 4*(6), 365–383.

Berry, J. W. (1980). Acculturation as varieties of adaptation. In A. M. Padilla (Ed.), *Acculturation: Theory, models, and some new findings* (pp. 9–25). Boulder, CO: Westview Press.

Berry, J. W. (2003). Conceptual approaches to acculturation. In K. M. Chun, P. B. Organista, & G. Marin (Eds.), *Acculturation: Advances in theory, measurement, and applied research* (pp. 17–37). Washington, DC: American Psychological Association.

Berry, J. W. (2006a). Contexts of acculturation. In D. L. Sam & J. W. Berry (Eds.), *The Cambridge handbook of acculturation psychology* (pp. 27–42). New York, NY: Cambridge University Press.

Berry, J. W. (2006b). Stress perspectives on acculturation. In D. L. Sam & J. W. Berry (Eds.), *The Cambridge handbook of acculturation psychology* (pp. 43–57). New York, NY: Cambridge University Press.

Berry, J. W., Kim, U., Power, S., Young, M., & Bujaki, M. (1989). Acculturation attitudes in plural societies. *Applied Psychology, 38*, 185–206.

Berry, J. W., Phinney, J. S., Sam, D. L., & Vedder, P. (Eds.). (2006). *Immigrant youth in cultural transition: Acculturation, identity, and adaptation across national contexts*. Mahwah, NJ: Lawrence Erlbaum Associates Publishers.

Berry, J. W., Westin, C., Virta, E., Vedder, P., Rooney, R., & Sang, D. (2006). Design of the study: Selecting societies of settlement and immigrant groups. In J. W. Berry, J. S. Phinney, D. L. Sam, & P. Vedder (Eds.), *Immigrant youth in cultural transition: Acculturation, identity, and adaptation across national contexts* (pp. 15–45). Mahwah, NJ: Lawrence Erlbaum Associates Publishers.

Birman, D., & Simon, C. D. (2014). Acculturation research: Challenges, complexities, and possibilities. In F. L. Leong, L. Comas-Díaz, G. C. Nagayama Hall, V. C. McLoyd, & J. E. Trimble (Eds.), *APA handbook of multicultural psychology, Vol. 1: Theory and research* (pp. 207–230). Washington, DC: American Psychological Association. https://doi.org/10.1037/14189-011.

Bonilla-Silva, E. (2000). "This is a White Country": The racial ideology of the Western nations of the world-system. *Sociological Inquiry, 70*(2), 188–214.

Branscombe, N. R., Ellemers, N., Spears, R., & Doosje, B. (1999). The context and content of social identity threat. In N. Ellemers, R. Spears, & B. Doosje (Eds.), *Social identity: Context, commitment, and content* (pp. 35–58). Oxford, UK: Blackwell.

Callens, M. S. (2015). *Integration policies and public opinion: In conflict or in harmony?* Brussels, BE: Migration Integration Policy Index. Retrieved from http://www.mipex.eu.

Castillo, L. G., & Caver, K. A. (2009). Expanding the concept of acculturation in Mexican American rehabilitation psychology research and practice. *Rehabilitation Psychology, 54*, 351–362. https://doi.org/10.1037/a0017801.

Cheong, P. H., Edwards, R., Goulbourne, H., & Solomos, J. (2007). Immigration, social cohesion and social capital: A critical review. *Critical Social Policy, 27*(1), 24–49. https://doi.org/10.1177/0261018307072206.

Chomsky, N., & Barsamian, D. (1994). *The Prosperous few and the restless many.* Tucson, AZ: Odonian Press.

Costa, D. L., & Kahn, M. E. (2003). Civic engagement and community heterogeneity: An economist's perspective. *Perspectives on Politics, 1(1),* 103–111.

Dawkins, C. J. (2008). Outlook: Two views on Robert D. Putnam's "E Pluribus Unum: Diversity and community in the twenty-first century the 2006 Johan Skytte prize lecture": Reflections on diversity and social capital: A critique of Robert D. Putnam's "E Pluribus Unum: Diversity and community in the twenty-first century the 2006 Johan Skytte prize lecture". *Housing Policy Debate, 19(1),* 207–217. https://doi.org/10.1080/10511482.2008.9521631.

Den Hartog, D. N. (2004). Assertiveness. In R. J. House, P. J. Hanges, M. Javidan, P. W. Dofrman, & V. Gupta (Eds.), *Culture, leadership, and organizations: The GLOBE Study of 62 societies* (pp. 395–436). Thousand Oaks: Sage.

Diez Roux, A. (2007). Neighborhoods and health: Where are we and where do we go from here? *Revue D'epidemiologie Et De Sante Publique, 55(1),* 13–21.

Diez-Roux, R. A. (2003). The examination of neighborhood effects on health: Conceptual and methodological issues related to the presence of multiple levels of organization. In I. Kawachi & L. F. Berkman (Eds.), *Neighborhoods and health* (pp. 45–64). New York, NY: Oxford.

Dovidio, J. F., Gaertner, S. L., & Esses, V. M. (2008). Cooperation, common identity, and intergroup contact. In B. A. Sullivan, M. Snyder, & J. L. Sullivan (Eds.), *Cooperation: The political psychology of effective human interaction* (pp. 143–159). Oxford, UK: Blackwell.

Dovidio, J. F., Gaertner, S. L., & Kafati, G. (2000). Group identity and intergroup relations: The common in-group identity model. In S. R. Thye, E. J. Lawler, M. W. Macy, & H. A. Walker (Eds.), *Advances in group processes* (Vol. 17, pp. 1–34). Stamford, CT: JAI Press.

Downey, L. (2006). Using geographic information systems to reconceptualize spatial relationships and ecological context. *American Journal of Sociology, 112(2),* 567–612. https://doi.org/10.1086/506418.

Ellemers, N., & Haslam, S. A. (2012). Social identity theory. In P. A. M. Van Lange, A. W. Kruglanski, & E. T. Higgins (Eds.), *Handbook of theories of social psychology* (pp. 379–398). Thousand Oaks, CA: Sage.

Elliott, D., Mayadas, N. S., & Segal, U. A. (2010). Immigration worldwide: Trends and analysis. In U. A. Segal, D. Elliot, & N. S. Mayadas (Eds.), *Immigration worldwide: Policies, practices, and trends* (pp. 17–26). New York, NY: Oxford.

Fischer, R. (2014). What values can (and cannot) tell us about individuals, society, and culture. In M. J. Gelfand, C. Chiu, Y. Hong, M. J. Gelfand, C. Chiu, & Y. Hong (Eds.), *Advances in culture and psychology* (pp. 218–272). New York, NY: Oxford University Press.

Gaertner, S. L., & Dovidio, J. F. (2000). *Reducing intergroup bias: The common ingroup identity model.* New York, NY: Taylor & Francis.

Gaertner, S. L., & Dovidio, J. F. (2012). The common ingroup identity model. In P. A. M. Van Lange, A. W. Kruglanski, & E. T. Higgins (Eds.), *Handbook of theories of social psychology* (pp. 439–457). Thousand Oaks, CA: Sage.

Gaertner, S. L., Rust, M. C., Dovidio, J. F., Bachman, B. A., & Anastasio, P. A. (1996). The contact hypothesis: The role of a common ingroup identity on reducing intergroup bias among majority and minority group members. In J. L. Nye & A. M. Brower (Eds.), *What's social about social cognition?* (pp. 230–360). Newbury Park, CA: Sage Publications.

Garcia-Retamero, R., Müller, S. M., & Rousseau, D. L. (2012). The impact of value similarity and power on the perception of threat. *Political Psychology, 33*(2), 179–193. https://doi.org/10.1111/j.1467-9221.2012.00869.x.

Gelfand, M., Raver, J. L., Nishii, L., Leslie, L. A., Lun, J., Lim, B. C., … Yamaguchi, S. (2011). Differences between tight and loose cultures: A 33-nation study. *Science, 332*(6033), 1100–1104. https://doi.org/10.1126/science.1197754.

Gelfand, M. J., Bhawuk, D. P. S., Nishi, L. H., & Bechtold, D. J. (2004). Individualism and collectivism. In R. J. House, P. J. Hanges, M. Javidan, P. W. Dorfman, & V. Gupta (Eds.), *Culture, leadership, and organizations: The GLOBE Study of 62 societies* (pp. 437–512). Thousand Oaks, CA: Sage.

Gupta, V., & Hanges, P. J. (2004). Regional and climate clustering of societal cultures. In R. J. House, P. J. Hanges, M. Javidan, P. W. Dorfman, & V. Gupta (Eds.), *Culture, leadership, and organizations: The GLOBE Study of 62 societies* (pp. 178–218). Thousand Oaks, CA: Sage.

Hanges, P. J., & Dickson, M. W. (2004). The development and validation of the GLOBE Culture and Leadership scales. In R. J. House, P. J. Hanges, M. Javidan, P. W. Dorfman, & V. Gupta (Eds.), *Culture, leadership, and organizations: The GLOBE Study of 62 societies* (pp. 122–151). Thousand Oaks, CA: Sage.

Hanges, P. J., Dickson, M. W., & Sipe, M. T. (2004). Rationale for GLOBE societies and application of test banding. In R. J. House, P. J. Hanges, M. Javidan, P. W. Dorfman, & V. Gupta (Eds.), *Culture, leadership, and organizations: The GLOBE Study of 62 societies* (pp. 219–233). Thousand Oaks, CA: Sage.

Heine, S. J. (2012). *Cultural psychology* (2nd ed.). New York, NY: Norton.

Hewstone, M., Floe, C., Al Ramiah, A., Schmid, K., Son, E., Wolfer, R., & Lolliot, S. (2015). Diversity and intergroup contact in schools. In R. Koopmans, B. Lancee, & M. Schaeffer (Eds.), *Social cohesion and immigration in Europe and North America* (pp. 208–228). New York, NY: Routledge.

Hofstede, G. (1980). *Culture's consequences: International differences in work-related values*. London: Sage.

House, R. J. (2004). Illustrative examples of GLOBE findings. In R. J. House, P. J. Hanges, M. Javidan, P. W. Dofrman, & V. Gupta (Eds.), *Culture, leadership, and organizations: The GLOBE Study of 62 societies* (pp. 3–8). Thousand Oaks, CA: Sage.

House, R. J., Hanges, P. J., Javidan, M., Dorfman, P. W., & Gupta, V. (Eds.). (2004). *Culture, leadership, and organizations: The GLOBE Study of 62 societies.* Thousand Oaks, CA: Sage.

House, R. J., & Hanges, P. J. (2004). Research design. In R. J. House, P. J. Hanges, M. Javidan, P. W. Dorfman, & V. Gupta (Eds.), *Culture, leadership, and organizations: The GLOBE Study of 62 societies* (pp. 95–101). Thousand Oaks, CA: Sage.

House, R. J., & Javidan, M. (2004). Overview of GLOBE. In R. J. House, P. J. Hanges, M. Javidan, P. W. Dofrman, & V. Gupta (Eds.), *Culture, leadership, and organizations: The GLOBE Study of 62 societies* (pp. 9–28). Thousand Oaks, CA: Sage.

Human Rights Watch. (2017). *World report: Events of 2016.* Retrieved from https://www.hrw.org/sites/default/files/world_report_download/wr2017-web.pdf

Huo, Y. J., Smith, H. J., Tyler, T. R., & Lind, E. A. (1996). Superordinate identification, subgroup identification, and justice concerns: Is separatism the problem; Is assimilation the answer? *Psychological Science, 7*(1), 40–45.

Javidan, M. (2004). Performance Orientation. In R. J. House, P. J. Hanges, M. Javidan, P. W. Dofrman, & V. Gupta (Eds.), *Culture, leadership, and organizations: The GLOBE Study of 62 societies* (pp. 239–281). Thousand Oaks, CA: Sage.

Javidan, M., & Hauser, M. (2004). The linkage between GLOBE findings and other cross-cultural information. In R. J. House, P. J. Hanges, M. Javidan, P. W. Dofrman, & V. Gupta (Eds.), *Culture, leadership, and organizations: The GLOBE Study of 62 societies* (pp. 102–121). Thousand Oaks, CA: Sage.

Javidan, M., House, R. J., & Dorfman, P. W. (2004). A non-technical summary of GLOBE findings. In R. J. House, P. J. Hanges, M. Javidan, P. W. Dofrman, & V. Gupta (Eds.), *Culture, leadership, and organizations: The GLOBE Study of 62 societies* (pp. 29–48). Thousand Oaks, CA: Sage.

Johnston, R., Poulsen, M., & Forrest, J. (2007). The geography of ethnic residential segregation: A comparative study of five countries. *Annals of the Association of American Geographers, 97*(4), 713–738. https://doi.org/10.1111/j.1467-8306.2007.00579.x.

Juang, L. P., & Cookston, J. T. (2009). Acculturation, discrimination, and depressive symptoms among Chinese American adolescents: A longitudinal study. *The Journal of Primary Prevention, 30*(3–4), 475–496. https://doi.org/10.1007/s10935-009-0177-9.

Kabasakal, H., & Bodur, M. (2004). Humane orientation in societies, organizations, and leader attributes. In R. J. House, P. J. Hanges, M. Javidan, P. W. Dofrman, & V. Gupta (Eds.), *Culture, leadership, and organizations: The GLOBE Study of 62 societies* (pp. 564–601). Thousand Oaks, CA: Sage.

Kim, B. S. K., & Abreu, J. M. (2001). Acculturation measurement: Theory, current instruments, and future directions. In J. G. Ponterotto, J. M. Casas, L. A.

Suzuki, & C. M. Alexander (Eds.), *Handbook of multicultural counseling* (2nd ed., pp. 394–424). Thousand Oaks, CA: Sage.

Kim, B. S. K., & Alamilla, S. G. (2017). Ethnic minority psychology: Perspectives on assimilation and acculturation. In A. Blume (Ed.), *Social issues in living color: Challenges and solutions from the perspective of ethnic minority psychology* (pp. 25–52). Santa Barbara: Praeger Books.

Kim, B. S. K., Li, L. C., & Ng, G. F. (2005). Asian American values scale – multidimensional: Development, reliability, and validity. *Cultural Diversity and Ethnic Minority Psychology, 11*, 187–201.

Kim, B. S. K., & Omizo, M. M. (2005). Asian and European American cultural values, collective self-esteem, acculturative stress, cognitive flexibility, and general self-efficacy among Asian American college students. *Journal of Counseling Psychology, 52*, 412–419. https://doi.org/10.1037/0022-0167.52.3.412.

Kim, B. S. K., & Omizo, M. M. (2006). Behavioral acculturation and enculturation and psychological functioning among Asian American college students. *Cultural Diversity and Ethnic Minority Psychology, 12*, 245–258. https://doi.org/10.1037/1099-9809.12.2.245.

Kim, B. S. K., & Omizo, M. M. (2010). Behavioral enculturation and acculturation, psychological functioning, and help-seeking attitudes among Asian American adolescents. *Asian American Journal of Psychology, 1*, 175–185. https://doi.org/10.1037/a0021125.

Kim, B. S. K., Soliz, A., Orellana, B., & Alamilla, S. G. (2009). Latino/a values scale: Development, reliability, and validity. *Measurement and Evaluation in Counseling and Development, 42*(2), 71–91.

Kitayama, S., Duffy, S., & Uchida, Y. (2007). Self as cultural mode of being. In S. Kitayama & D. Cohen (Eds.), *Handbook of cultural psychology* (pp. 136–174). New York, NY: Guilford Press.

Koopmans, R. (2013). Multiculturalism and immigration: A contested field in cross-national comparison. *Annual Review of Sociology, 39*, 147–169. https://doi.org/10.1146/annurev-soc-071312-145630.

Koopmans, R., & Veit, S. (2014). Cooperation in ethnically diverse neighborhoods: A lost-letter experiment. *Political Psychology, 35*(3), 379–400. https://doi.org/10.1111/pops.12037.

Koopmans, R., Lancee, B., & Schaeffer, M. (2015). Ethnic diversity in diverse societies. In R. Koopmans, B. Lancee, & M. Schaeffer (Eds.), *Social cohesion and immigration in Europe and North America* (pp. 1–19). New York, NY: Routledge.

Krause, M., & Montenegro, C. R. (2017). Community as a multifaceted concept. In M. A. Bond, I. Serrano-Garcia, & C. B. Keys (Eds.), *APA handbook of community psychology: Volume 1. Theoretical foundations, core concepts, and emerging challenges* (pp. 275–294). Washington, DC: American Psychological Association. https://doi.org/10.1037/14953-013.

Lancee, B., & Schaeffer, M. (2015). Moving to diversity: Residential mobility, changes in ethnic diversity, and concerns about immigration. In R. Koopmans, B. Lancee, & M. Schaeffer (Eds.), *Social cohesion and immigration in Europe and North America* (pp. 38–55). New York, NY: Routledge.

Landis, D., & Albert, R. D. (2012). Introduction: Models and theories of ethnic conflict. In D. Landis, R. D. Albert, D. Landis, & R. D. Albert (Eds.), *Handbook of ethnic conflict: International perspectives* (pp. 1–17). New York, NY: Springer Science. https://doi.org/10.1007/978-1-4614-0448-4_1.

Laurence, J. (2011). The effect of ethnic diversity and community disadvantage on social cohesion: A multi-level analysis of social capital and interethnic relations in UK communities. *European Sociological Review, 27*, 70–89. https://doi.org/10.1093/esr/jcp057.

Laurence, J., & Heath, A. (2008). *Predictors of community cohesion: Multi-level modelling of the 2005 Citizenship Survey.* London, UK: Department for Communities and Local Government.

Lazarsfeld, P. F., & Merton, R. K. (1954). Friendship as a social process: A substantive and methodological analysis. In M. Berger (Ed.), *Freedom and control in modern society* (pp. 18–66). New York, NY: Van Nostrand.

Maly, M. T. (2005). *Beyond segregation: Multiracial and multiethnic neighborhoods in the United States.* Philadelphia, PA: Temple University Press.

Markus, H. R., & Kitayama, S. (1991). Culture and the self: Implications for cognition, emotions, and motivation. *Psychological Review, 98*(2), 224–253.

Massey, D. S., & Denton, N. A. (1993). *American apartheid: Segregation and the making of the underclass.* Cambridge, MA: Harvard University Press.

Massey, D. S., Rothwell, J., & Domina, T. (2009). The changing bases of segregation in the United States. *American Academy of Political and Social Science, 626*(1), 74–90. https://doi.org/10.1177/0002716209343558.

McPherson, M., Smith-Lovin, L., & Cook, J. M. (2001). Birds of a feather: Homophily in social networks. *Annual Review of Sociology, 27*, 415–444. https://doi.org/10.1146/annurev.soc.27.1.415.

Migration Integration Policy Index. (2015). *How countries are promoting integration of immigrants* [Website]. Retrieved from http://www.mipex.eu/key-findings

Milanovic, B. (2016). *Global inequality: A new approach for the age of globalization.* Cambridge, MA: Harvard University Press.

Neal, Z. P., & Watling Neal, J. (2014). The (in)compatibility of diversity and sense of community. *American Journal of Community Psychology, 53*(1–2), 1–12. https://doi.org/10.1007/s10464-013-9608-0.

Nguyen, H. H. (2006). Acculturation in the United States. In D. L. Sam & J. W. Berry (Eds.), *The Cambridge handbook of acculturation psychology* (pp. 311–330). New York, NY: Cambridge University Press.

Obasi, E. M., & Leong, F. T. L. (2010). Construction and validation of the Measurement Acculturation Strategies for People of African Descent (MASPAD). *Cultural Diversity and Ethnic Minority Psychology, 16*(4), 526–539. https://doi.org/10.1037/a0021374.

Okamoto, D., & Mora, G. C. (2014). Panethnicity. *Annual Review of Sociology, 40*, 219–239. https://doi.org/10.1146/annurev-soc-071913-043201.

Oliver, J. E. (2010). *The paradox of integration: Race, neighborhood, and civic life in multiethnic America*. Chicago, IL: The University of Chicago Press.

Oliver, J. E., & Ha, S. E. (2008). The segregation paradox: Neighborhoods and interracial contact in multiethnic America. In B. A. Sullivan, M. Snyder, & J. L. Sullivan (Eds.), *Cooperation: The political psychology of effective human interaction* (pp. 161–180). Oxford, UK: Blackwell.

Organista, P. B., Marin, G., & Chun, K. M. (2010). *The psychology of ethnic groups in the United States*. Thousand Oaks, CA: Sage.

Oyserman, D., Coon, H. M., & Kemmelmeier, M. (2002). Rethinking individualism and collectivism: Evaluation of theoretical assumptions and meta-analyses. *Psychological Bulletin, 128*(1), 3–72. https://doi.org/10.1037/0033-2909.128.1.3.

Oyserman, D., & Yoon, K.-I. (2009). Neighborhood effects on racial–ethnic identity: The undermining role of segregation. *Race and Social Problems, 1*(2), 67–76. https://doi.org/10.1007/s12552-009-9007-1.

Pettigrew, T. F., & Tropp, L. R. (2006). A meta-analytic test of Intergroup Contract Theory. *Journal of Personality and Social Psychology, 90*(5), 751–783. https://doi.org/10.1037/0022-3514.90.5.751.

Pettigrew, T. F., Wagner, U., & Christ, O. (2010). Population ratios and prejudice: Modelling both contact and threat effects. *Journal of Ethnic and Migration Studies, 36*(4), 635–650. https://doi.org/10.1080/13691830903516034.

Pew Research Center. (2015). *Modern immigration wave brings 59 million to U.S., driving population growth and change through 2065: Views of immigration's impact on U.S. society mixed*. Washington, DC: Author. Retrieved from http://www.pewhispanic.org/2015/09/28/modern-immigration-wave-brings-59-million-to-u-s-driving-population-growth-and-change-through-2065/

Phinney, J. S., Berry, J. W., Vedder, P., & Liebkind, K. (2006). The acculturation experience: Attitudes, identities, and behavior of immigrant youth. In J. W. Berry, J. S. Phinney, J. D. L. Sam, & P. Vedder (Eds.), *Immigrant youth in cultural transition: Acculturation, identity, and adaptation across national contexts* (pp. 71–116). Mahwah, NJ: Lawrence Erlbaum Associates Publishers.

Phinney, J. S., Jacoby, B., & Silva, C. (2007). Positive intergroup attitudes: The role of ethnic identity. *International Journal of Behavioral Development, 31*(5), 478–490. https://doi.org/10.1177/0165025407081466.

Pierce, S. J. (2010). *Using geostatistical models to study neighborhood effects: An alternative to hierarchical linear models* (Unpublished doctoral dissertation). Michigan State University, East Lansing, MI.

Portes, A. (1998). Social capital: Its origins and applications in modern sociology. *Annual Review of Sociology, 24*, 1–24. https://doi.org/10.1146/annurev.soc.24.1.

Portes, A., & Rumbaut, R. G. (2001). *Legacies: The story of the immigrant second generation.* Los Angeles, CA: University of California Press.

Portes, A., & Vickstrom, E. (2011). Diversity, social capital, and cohesion. *Annual Review of Sociology, 37*, 461–479. https://doi.org/10.1146/annurev-soc-081309-150022.

Prodi, R. (2004). Foreword. In R. Ingelhart, M. Basanez, J. Diez-Medrano, L. Halman, & R. Luijkx (Eds.), *Human beliefs and values* (pp. xiii–xvii). Mexico City, Mexico: Siglo XXI Editores.

Putnam, R. D. (2000). *Bowling alone: The collapse and revival of American community.* New York: Simon & Schuster.

Putnam, R. D. (2001). Foreword. In S. Saegert, J. P. Thompson, & M. R. Warren (Eds.), *Social capital and poor communities* (pp. xv–xvi). New York, NY: Russell Sage.

Putnam, R. D. (2007). E Pluribus Unum: Diversity and community in the twenty-first century The 2006 Johan Skytte Prize Lecture. *Scandinavian Political Studies, 30*(2), 137–174. https://doi.org/10.1111/j.1467-9477.2007.00176.x.

Radcliff, B. (2008). The politics of human happiness. In B. A. Sullivan, M. Snyder, & J. L. Sullivan (Eds.), *Cooperation: The political psychology of effective human interaction* (pp. 305–321). Oxford, UK: Blackwell.

Raudenbush, S. W., & Sampson, R. J. (1999). "Ecometrics": Toward a science of assessing ecological settings, with application to the systematic social observation of neighborhoods. *Sociological Methodology, 29*, 1–41.

Realo, A., Allik, J., & Greenfield, B. (2008). Radius of trust: Social capital in relation to familism and institutional collectivism. *Journal of Cross-Cultural Psychology, 39*(4), 447–462.

Realo, A., & Beilmann, M. (2012). Individualism-collectivism and social capital at the individual level. *Trames: Journal of the Humanities and Social Sciences, 16*(3), 205. https://doi.org/10.3176/tr.2012.3.01.

Redfield, R., Linton, R., & Herskovits, M. (1936). Memorandum on the study of acculturation. *American Anthropologist, 38*, 149–152.

Roth, K. (2017). The dangerous rise of populism: Global attacks on human rights values. In *Human Rights Watch, World report: Events of 2016* (pp. 1–14). New York, NY: Seven Stories Press. Retrieved from https://www.hrw.org/sites/default/files/world_report_download/wr2017-web.pdf.

Roy, A. L., Hughes, D., & Yoshikawa, H. (2012). Exploring neighborhood effects on health and life satisfaction: Disentangling neighborhood racial density and neighborhood income. *Race and Social Problems, 4*, 193–204. https://doi. org/10.1007/s12552-012-9079-1.

Rupasingha, A., Goetz, S. J., & Freshwater, D. (2006). The production of social capital in U.S. counties. *The Journal of Socio-Economics, 35*, 83–101.

Saegert, S., & Carpiano, R. M. (2017). Social support and social capital: A theoretical synthesis using community psychology and community sociology approaches. In M. A. Bond, I. Serrano-Garcia, & C. B. Keys (Eds.), *APA handbook of community psychology: Volume 1. Theoretical foundations, core concepts, and emerging challenges* (pp. 295–314). Washington, DC: American Psychological Association. https://doi.org/10.1037/14953-014.

Saegert, S., Thompson, J. P., & Warren, M. R. (Eds.). (2001). *Social capital and poor communities*. New York, NY: Russell Sage.

Sampson, R. J. (2001). Crime and public safety: Insights from community-level perspectives on social capital. In S. Saegert, J. P. Thompson, & M. R. Warren (Eds.), *Social capital and poor communities* (pp. 89–114). New York, NY: Russell Sage Foundation.

Sampson, R. J., & Graif, C. (2009). Neighborhood social capital as differential social organization: Resident and leadership dimensions. *American Behavioral Scientist, 52*(11), 1579–1605. https://doi.org/10.1177/0002764209 331527.

Sampson, R. J., Morenoff, J. D., & Gannon-Rowley, T. (2002). Assessing "neighborhood effects": Social processes and new directions in research. *Annual Review of Sociology, 28*, 443–478. https://doi.org/10.1146/annurev. soc.28.110601.141114.

Sampson, R. J., Raudenbush, S. W., & Earls, F. (1997). Neighborhoods and violent crime: A multilevel study of collective efficacy. *Science, 277*, 918–924. https://doi.org/10.1126/science.277.5328.918.

Schmid, K., Hewstone, M., & Al Ramiah, A. (2015). Diversity, trust, and intergroup attitudes: Underlying processes and mechanisms. In R. Koopmans, B. Lancee, & M. Schaeffer (Eds.), *Social cohesion and immigration in Europe and North America* (pp. 38–55). New York, NY: Routledge.

Schwartz, S. H. (1992). Universals in the content and structure of values: Theoretical advances and empirical tests in 20 countries. In M. P. Zanna & M. P. Zanna (Eds.), *Advances in experimental social psychology* (Vol. 25, pp. 1–65). San Diego, CA: Academic Press. https://doi.org/10.1016/ S0065-2601(08)60281-6.

Schwartz, S. H. (1994). Beyond individualism and collectivism: New cultural dimensions of values. In U. Kim, H. C. Triandis, C. Kagitçibasi, S. C. Choi, & G. Yoon (Eds.), *Individualism and collectivism: Theory, method, and applications* (pp. 85–119). London, UK: Sage.

Schwartz, S. J., Weisskirch, R. S., Hurley, E. A., Zamboanga, B. L., Park, I. K., Kim, S. Y., ... Greene, A. D. (2010). Communalism, familism, and filial piety: Are they birds of a collectivist feather? *Cultural Diversity and Ethnic Minority Psychology, 16*(4), 548–560. https://doi.org/10.1037/a0021370.

Simpson, H. E. (1949). Measurement of diversity. *Nature, 163*(4148), 688.

Smith, R. A. (1993). Creating stable racially integrated communities: A review. *Journal of Urban Affairs, 15*(2), 115–140.

Sullivan, B. A., Snyder, M., & Sullivan, J. L. (Eds.). (2008). *The political psychology of effective human interaction.* Oxford, UK: Blackwell.

Tajfel, H. (1970). Experiments in intergroup discrimination. *Scientific American, 223*, 96–102.

Tajfel, H., & Turner, J. C. (1979). An integrative theory of intergroup conflict. In W. G. Austin & S. Worchel (Eds.), *The social psychology of intergroup relations* (pp. 33–48). Monterrey, CA: Brooks/Cole.

Telles, E. E., & Ortiz, V. (2008). *Generations of exclusion: Mexican Americans, assimilation, and race.* New York, NY: Russell Sage.

Thoits, P. A. (2010). Sociological approaches to mental illness. In T. L. Scheid & T. N. Brown (Eds.), *A handbook for the study of mental health: Social contexts, theories, and systems* (2nd ed., pp. 106–124). New York, NY: Cambridge.

Thoits, P. A. (2013). Self, identity, stress, and mental health. In C. S. Aneshensel, J. C. Phelan, & A. Bierman (Eds.), *Handbook of the sociology of mental health* (2nd ed., pp. 357–377). New York, NY: Springer. https://doi.org/10.1007/978-94-007-4276-5_18.

Tov, W., & Diener, E. (2008). The well-being of nations: Linking together trust, cooperation, and democracy. In B. A. Sullivan, M. Snyder, & J. L. Sullivan (Eds.), *Cooperation: The political psychology of effective human interaction* (pp. 323–342). Oxford, UK: Blackwell.

Townley, G., Kloos, B., Green, E. P., & Franco, M. M. (2011). Reconcilable differences? Human diversity, cultural relativity, and sense of community. *American Journal of Community Psychology, 47*(1–2), 69–85. https://doi.org/10.1007/s10464-010-9379-9.

Triandis, H. C. (1994). *Culture and social behavior.* New York, NY: McGraw-Hill.

Triandis, H. C. (1995). *Individualism and collectivism.* Boulder, CO: Westview.

Triandis, H. C., & Gelfand, M. J. (2012). A theory of individualism and collectivism. In P. A. M. Van Lange, A. W. Kruglanski, & E. T. Higgins (Eds.), *Handbook of theories of social psychology* (pp. 495–520). Thousand Oaks, CA: Sage.

Triandis, H. C., Leung, K., Villareal, M. J., & Clack, F. L. (1985). Allocentric versus idiocentric tendencies: Convergent and discriminant validation. *Journal of Research in Personality, 19*, 395–415.

van de Vijver, F. J., & Matsumoto, D. (2012). Introduction to the methodological issues associated with cross-cultural research. In F. J. van de Vijver &

D. Matsumoto (Eds.), *Cross-cultural research methods in psychology* (pp. 1–14). New York, NY: Cambridge.

van der Meer, T., & Tolsma, J. (2014). Ethnic diversity and its effects on social cohesion. *Annual Review of Sociology, 40,* 459–478. https://doi.org/10.1146/annurev-soc-071913-043309.

van Oudenhoven, J. P. (2006). Immigrants. In D. L. Sam & J. W. Berry (Eds.), *The Cambridge handbook of acculturation psychology* (pp. 163–180). Cambridge: Cambridge University Press.

Veit, S. (2015). Thinking about ethnic diversity: Experimental evidence on the causal role of ethnic diversity in German neighborhoods and schools. In R. Koopmans, B. Lancee, & M. Schaeffer (Eds.), *Social cohesion and immigration in Europe and North America: Mechanisms, conditions, and causality* (pp. 167–186). New York, NY: Routledge.

Wagner, U., Christ, O., Pettigrew, T. F., Stellmacher, J., & Wolf, C. (2006). Prejudice and minority proportion: Contact instead of threat effects. *Social Psychology Quarterly, 69*(4), 380–390.

Walton, E., & Hardebeck, M. (2016). Multiethnic neighborhoods on the ground. *Du Bois Review: Social Science Research on Race, 13*(2), 345–363. https://doi.org/10.1017/S1742058X16000230.

Warren, M. R., Thompson, J. P., & Saegert, S. (2001). The role of social capital in combating poverty. In S. Saegert, J. P. Thompson, & M. R. Warren (Eds.), *Social capital and poor communities* (pp. 1–28). New York, NY: Russell Sage.

Williams, D. R., & Collins, C. (2002a). Racial residential segregation: A fundamental cause of racial disparities in health. In T. A. LaVeist (Ed.), *Race, ethnicity, and health: A public health reader* (pp. 369–390). San Francisco, CA: Wiley.

Williams, D. R., & Collins, C. (2002b). US socioeconomic and racial differences in health: Patterns and explanations. In T. A. LaVeist (Ed.), *Race, ethnicity, and health: A public health reader* (pp. 391–431). San Francisco, CA: Wiley.

Wilson, W. J., & Taub, R. (2006). *There goes the neighborhood: Racial, ethnic, and class. Tensions in four Chicago neighborhoods and their meaning for America.* New York, NY: Alfred A. Knopf.

Woolf, S. H., & Aron, L. (2013). *U.S. health in international perspective: Shorter lives, poorer health.* Washington, DC: National Academies Press.

Zea, M. C., Asner-Self, K. K., Birman, D., & Buki, L. P. (2003). The abbreviated multidimensional acculturation scale: Empirical validation with two Latino/Latina samples. *Cultural Diversity and Ethnic Minority Psychology, 9,* 107–126. https://doi.org/10.1037/1099-9809.9.2.107.

CHAPTER 6

The *Social Contract Theory* Revisited: Examining the Relationship Between Greed, Conflict, and the Evolution of Cooperation

In the last several chapters we have discussed causal factors associated with the psychological, political, environmental, and socioevolutionary impact of violence, ethnic conflict, and aggression. While conflict may *appear* to be an inherent and universal trait that is characteristic of human interaction, there are many things that communities can do to help improve our understanding of one another and facilitate growth by providing networks of contact, cooperation, and communication which ultimately may reduce its prevalence. Individualistic cultures that emphasize competition, winning within a "zero-sum" context (i.e., "If I win, you must lose") of human interaction remains a growing universal and global phenomenon that also has been identified to be a contributing factor to aggression and conflict (Santos, Varnum, & Grossman, 2017). On a more positive note, we have also explored the psychodynamics of human engagement, interaction, and communication, and how the role of community development can play an instrumental role in not only reducing the likelihood of conflict and group violence, but perhaps, more importantly, how a variety of community service activities may facilitate understanding, growth, and communication among groups that have been historically and diametrically opposed to one another.

© The Author(s) 2018   135
A. J. Hoffman et al., *The Role of Community Development
in Reducing Extremism and Ethnic Conflict*,
https://Doi.org/10.1007/978-3-319-75699-8_6

The Philosophy of Human Nature, Egoism, and the Social Contract

In this final chapter we will also explore how early political philosophers and the British empiricists (i.e., John Locke, Thomas Hobbes, and Jean Jacques Rousseau) described human nature as complex in that humans typically possess a broad range of mutually exclusive and even contradictory traits, exhibiting both egoistic, opportunistic behavior and prosocial, altruistic behavior. Rousseau and Locke also argued (given the inherent contradictions of human behaviors) that the rules of governments and communities must remain cognizant of this behavioral dichotomy and need to strike a balance in providing ample opportunities for people to work cooperatively within their community despite each person harboring an uncivilized, animalistic "savage state" that Hobbes referred to as a "state of nature."[1] The state of nature refers to the basic instincts of human nature and natural behaviors prior to the existence of any civilized society that contains rules and laws governing human behaviors. Both Hobbes and Rousseau argue that indeed given the natural state of humanity, humans exist in a highly opportunistic and egoistic state, maximizing their pleasures typically at the expense (and exploitation) of others. Given the raw and animalistic nature that all humans share, some form or means of laws must exist in order for groups and communities to exist. Despite our highly egoistic and animalistic nature, the early political philosophers such as Thomas Hobbes, John Locke, and Jean Jacques Rousseau also believed that humans are rational creatures and are quite capable of living in order and through a democratically based system of laws.

Hobbes argued in *Leviathan* (published in 1651 during the English Civil War) that the behavior among humans was complex yet predictable, not uncommon during an era that promoted the systematic and mechanistic nature of human behaviors. In *Leviathan*, Hobbes argues that given the ruthless nature of humanity where all people want all things for themselves, civilization would be impossible without some form of government monitoring individual behaviors. The rule of law, however, would need to be determined by the majority of the people comprising any given territory acknowledging that some of these rights would need to be limited in order to make group living possible. The impetus of human behaviors was typically self-interest, one that maximized benefits to the self and typically

---

[1] https://plato.stanford.edu/entries/hobbes-moral/.

exploited others. According to Hobbes, a community existing of egoistic and self-interested individuals simply could not be possible without some overarching authority that governed behaviors, such as a monarchy or king. According to the political philosophical perspectives of Hobbes, Locke, and Rousseau, all persons *do* have the capacity to engage in a rational dialogue with each other to facilitate civil harmony and social discourse, but how a community or society is structured with rules and laws will determine if this rational dialogue and civilization are even possible. While Hobbes was less optimistic of individuals capable of cooperation and exercising their freedoms given their savage state of nature, John Locke argued that the freedoms shared by members of a community are only possible through the development of a civil and democratic government that justified the rejection of a totalitarian monarchy (i.e., "King") and recognized the rights for individuals (i.e., owning property).

In his now-famous quotation "Man is born free ... but lives his life in chains," Rousseau raises the difficult question of how groups of individuals may experience a true sense of community while simultaneously recognizing the true savage ("state of nature"), egoistic disposition of humanity and the need in sharing the mundane responsibilities that make a community healthy, productive, and viable. Rousseau also recognizes the universal tendency for humans to live within a hedonistic and self-centered world that maximizes individual pleasure, but that only through maturation and the development of civic responsibility, laws, and reason do we conclude that such a natural and desired life is impossible. If we wish to engage in some form of community interaction where commerce, trade, and even our very existence were possible, then our individual rights *ipso facto* must be both compromised and limited.

Although the basic components of the social contract theory dates back to the earliest of the Greek philosophers (i.e., Plato and Aristotle), more recently, Rousseau and Locke have argued that in order for any community or society to be economically viable and robust, governments must recognize the inherent selfish human nature that all persons possess with the need for rules and laws that govern society. In this sense, according to Rousseau, all individuals must *knowingly* relinquish and yield some of their rights in order that *all* persons within the community may live within a true democratic state. Rousseau (1762) argued that humans were considered more of the "noble savage" in defining our relationships with other individuals, which simply meant that while people are *capable* of living together without violence and conflict, the propensity and tendency for violence and greed among groups are always present. An inverse correlation exists between the number of individuals who happen to comprise in a given area and the degree to which individual freedom may be exercised. As membership within a community and overall populations increase, our individual rights and the privileges that we share proportionately decrease. Rousseau and Hobbes noted that even though humans are capable of rational and reasonable thought, our behaviors are inherently egoistic, opportunistic, and exploitative of the rights of others.

This predisposition to maximize inherent benefits that support our biological needs at the expense of others was what Hobbes refers to as "natural self-interest." Despite the tendency for humans to display universal traits of self-interest and greed, people still possess the capacity to engage in reason and rational thought that provides ideal living conditions within productive communities. This common need that we all share, despite recognizing our own selfish traits, can provide the impetus for all members within society to engage in a democratic and principled style of governance. The social contract recognizes that the needs of the group justify and outweigh the needs of the opportunistic individual, and that in order to live productively, we need to think and work both cooperatively and collectively. This common form of democracy whereby individuals live and work through an agreed-upon system of law was the antithesis of the monarchy that was common in England and, ultimately, developed into what Locke (2003) referred to as the "real foundation of society." Rousseau also rejected the so-called divine interpretation of ruling by monarchy and insisted that communities play a central role in governing the inherent selfish nature of humans. Nobility and respect within community engagement is achieved by denying ourselves of any advantage to secure goods by force, but rather through helping individuals defend their own rights in property and business. Democracy and political order therefore are things that do not come easily (nor are they inherent in human nature) but only exist through intentionality and shared governance in community development. The psychodynamics of intergroup contact help individuals to work and understand each other in a more equitable environment, and that increased cooperative exchanges among groups can enhance communication and reduce factors (i.e., oppression and prejudice) that have been associated with specific forms of violence and ethnic conflict.

The theories that were proposed by Hobbes, Locke, and Rousseau were truly visionary in that they identified the true essence and potential of human nature (i.e., the "savage state"), and that the capacity of human engagement and productivity depended on how laws within communities were constructed and established. Knowing how humans interact with each other based on their inherently egoistic nature and capacity for conflict necessitated the development of laws that were both equitable and reasonable. A most productive and humanitarian community is one that provides opportunities for all individuals to contribute their individuals skills and expertise in a fair, collaborative, and equitable process. It is a community where people *want* to share their skills and live in harmony with each other while also abiding by the democratically obtained laws that govern society. Recognizing that society and the essence of community development depend on the contributions of all persons working collaboratively and recognizing the laws that govern their behaviors, the ingredients of a productive environment were established that gradually inspired the discipline of modern community psychology.

COMMUNITY SERVICE ACTIVITIES AS EFFECTIVE METHODS IN BRIDGING CULTURAL DIVIDES

Despite the inherent universal evolutionary existence of greed and egoism, the role of community growth and development is dependent on each individual's awareness of the need to work cooperatively and collectively with others despite competing self-interests. As Rousseau and Hobbes noted in previous discussions, society and, more generally, civilization are dependent on our own awareness that some human rights must be compromised so that democracy itself may exist. More recently, scholars have noted the interesting relationship between voluntary activities, group trust, and community growth in the development of community gardening programs (Glover, Shinew, & Parry, 2005). Additionally, community gardens provide a unique outdoor environment that offers opportunities for individuals to engage with each other, share information, and support one another, which are instrumental in building what Glover and colleagues (2005) refer to as a form of "educative citizenship" (p. 80). This unique form of ecological group interaction can also facilitate democratic and collective decision-making processes that impact the entire community.

Recent research (Al Ramiah & Hewstone, 2013; Brown & Hewstone, 2005; Ellis & Abdi, 2017) has addressed direct methods (i.e., intergroup contact) and differentiating styles of group interaction (i.e., established social connection and "social linking") through the development of superordinate goals that have been successful in reducing conflict and bias that is directed toward out-group members such as Syrian refugees and Lebanese nationals (Saab, Harb, & Moughalian, 2017) and Mexicans living within the United States (Ridge & Montoya, 2013). The tools that have proven to be most successful in bridging gaps among ethnically diverse groups and improving levels of communication are both direct and tangible in that all groups share a responsibility in participating in a variety of community-based programs (i.e., community service work and community improvement stewardship programs). Similarly, recent research has identified the development of trust through community-based programs that help build social capital as a highly effective process in reducing extremism and ethnic conflict (Riley, 2013). Communities that are equipped to establish what Riley (2013) refers to as "community cohesion" (p. 270) can provide mechanisms in which groups representing different values and belief systems may help identify common ground in the process and direction in which communities develop. Furthermore, the concept of social capital has also been described as a type or form of "social energy" (p. 271) where diverse ethnic and religious groups can discuss their history and culture with other community members and identify common themes that help to reduce stigmas and fears that historically have provided the incentive to ethnic hate crimes.

The intergroup contact that occurs as a result of interactive and cooperative community service activities is precisely the mechanism that provides a forum and an environment conducive to communication with individuals from diverse backgrounds. Intergroup contact is a necessary (but non-sufficient) factor in the process of improving the understanding of the needs of diverse groups and reducing interethnic conflict. Individuals from diverse backgrounds not only require contact with each other (i.e., reduced polarization), but also need to be exposed to mutually beneficial superordinate goals in order to achieve group harmony. Stated more simply, people need an environment that provides opportunities of collective efforts in reaching a common goal. The collaboration among group members during the completion of community service activities and service work programs provides incentives for individuals from various economic, religious, and ethnic backgrounds to engage and communicate with each other as goals are achieved. More importantly, the increased exposure and interaction with diverse groups help to dispel and debunk the negative stereotypes that often are contributing factors to polarization and ethnic conflict (Al Ramiah & Hewstone, 2013; Pettigrew & Tropp, 2006).

Ellis and Abdi (2017) have identified several key factors in the development of community resilience, with "social connection" as the most vital component in helping members improve their communication with each other, increase trust, and establish relationships that help to promote social capital. Communities that have developed a stronger sense of resiliency are also highly effective in their efforts to reduce extremism and ethnic conflict by also reducing negative stereotypes associated with at-risk populations. Unfortunately, often when disaster (i.e., shootings or bomb attacks) strikes a community, the most vulnerable groups (ethnic minority groups) become scapegoated and unfairly blamed for the tragedy. Despite the fact that Muslim-Americans have committed significantly *fewer* hate crimes and acts of extremism than other groups (Miller, 2014), they remain targeted as "extremist groups" by the media, which perpetuates the negative stereotypes that are commonly associated with these groups (Ellis & Abdi, 2011). Islamophobia, ideology, and hate crimes directed against Muslim-Americans have all significantly increased in the post-9/11 era, creating a greater need today for communities to provide opportunities of engagement and interaction that will build trust and foster a sense of community identity.

COMMUNITIES IMPACTED BY TRAUMA AND VIOLENCE

Understanding the basic and inherent greed that all persons share but also realizing the capacity for shared governance and community growth became essential in the development of laws and governing systems within future societies. Providing communities that have been negatively impacted through acts of war (i.e., genocide and ethnic cleansing) and group/gang violence with a variety of resources (i.e., intervention and prevention programs) has been shown to be highly successful in helping residents develop a stronger sense of connectedness to their communities and interpersonal attachment to their community members (Agani, Landau, & Agani, 2010). In particular, one community intervention program identified as the *Linking Human Systems Community Resilience Model* (or LINC) has shown promise through combining collective support and identification of strengths and skills among individuals who have been exposed to group violence, trauma, and related problems (i.e., substance abuse) during the occupation of Kosovo between 1989 and 1999.[2] Helping communities

[2] The LINC program demonstrated the importance of maintaining cultural heritage among refugees who have been displaced in foreign countries and how resilience may be established when provided with resources to help cope with socioeconomic change.

redevelop, heal, and recuperate after a series of war crimes requires skilled intervention in recognizing the unique cultural and spiritual values that are held by the residents of that community.

Ferid Agani et al. (2010) have identified the importance of providing special community-based and preventative care to victims of trauma and war crimes during the Kosovo occupation. In particular, the LINC program took into consideration the unique qualities of this population while developing a treatment program, including the existence of enclaves and unique tight-knit extended family structures that often rejected any intervention from "outsiders." Counselors that are specially trained and equipped to treat victims of war crimes and trauma were effective in applying specific types of treatment and practice (i.e., family therapy) that are unique to their own culture and setting. It is this particular attention to the unique needs among victims based on different cultural practices and values that makes community-based treatments such as LINC most effective among vulnerable populations.

INTERGROUP CONTACT DRIVES BOTH COOPERATIVE AND PROSOCIAL BEHAVIORS

A central theme throughout this text has been the central role that community and social groups have in shaping various types of behaviors. If left unchecked, individuals within groups can superficially determine their preferences with others based on phenotypical characteristics (i.e., "they look more like me") and polarize themselves from the dominant group. Once several groups have become polarized, negative perceptions (i.e., stereotypes and false beliefs) develop that further distance and antagonize the relationships among different groups. When individuals perceive others to be more like them either from a political (i.e., political preferences, now commonly referred to as "identity politics"), economic, or religious perspective, they are significantly more likely to interact, identify, and socialize with them (Peterson & Dietz, 2005), with some exceptions involving low-status groups who tend to reject demographic similarity (Umphress, Smith-Crowe, Brief, Dietz, & Watkins, 2007).

A related theme addressing intergroup preferences associated with different social hierarchies has been referred to as social dominance theory (Sidanious & Pratto, 1999). According to this research, individuals who identify with specific cultural ideologies (i.e., meritocracy, capitalism, etc.) tend to support (or reject) social hierarchies that have been associated with (and justify) oppressive practices and unequal class-based behaviors. Eventually, one group will attempt to assert dominance (both economic and psychological) over other groups and in-group bias and conflict will ultimately result. We begin our discussion by maintaining that despite the universal tendency toward psychological dominance, all groups have the potential and capacity to coexist and work toward intergroup cooperation, harmony, and peace.

Research has shown that often intergroup conflict begins when several groups share the need for limited resources that are vital for human existence. A "zero-sum competitive relationship" (Gaertner et al. 2000) emerges, where individuals view others as threats to these resources rather than as cooperative agents working toward mutually beneficial goals. Once groups have become separated and perceived as threats to each other's own well-being, the process of categorization and social identity develops, which typically becomes exacerbated by negative stereotypes that are directed to out-group members. Eventually, as the bond of in-group membership becomes stronger, antipathy toward out-group members increases and conflict (both direct and indirect) usually develops.

Contact Hypothesis, the Internet, and Community Development Programs

Classic research (Gaertner and colleagues, 2000; Gaertner, Mann, Murrell, & Dovidio, 1989; Sheriff, Harvey, White, Hood, & Sherif, 1961) has shown how intergroup contact and the development of superordinate goals can help to debunk negative stereotypes while reducing intergroup conflict. Communities have a unique opportunity in preventing intergroup and ethnic conflict in reducing negative bias that is often attributed to minority groups through proactive development of programs that facilitate increased contact and superordinate goals. Recent research has identified an emerging tool that has powerful reach for virtually all populations in expanding contact theory and facilitating communication among interethnic groups within the community.

Yair Amichai-Hamburger and Katelyn Y. A. McKenna (2006) have described the internet as the most recent tool in which the contact theory may be implemented among various group members to help reduce various forms of conflict and increase communication within those groups. The internet has tremendous global application in that its use is universal and becoming increasingly available to most populations. Recent estimates place internet application at over three billion users, and this number continues to increase on a daily basis.[3] Part of the advantage of internet use is both the far-reaching capacity that it shares with all users and how the application is shared among users. Part of the limitations of the classic contact theory has been anxiety. Getting to know strangers from diverse cultures usually is difficult for people and has kept them from going outside of their "comfort zone" in establishing new friendships and relationships. An additional hurdle to overcome in classic contact theory has been the perception of *equality* among our peers. Individuals who perceive others as their equal counterpart are significantly more likely to establish a positive relationship and friendship as opposed to differences in economic, political, or religious ideologies (McClendon, 1974).

Internet use helps to overcome these two formidable problems proposed by Amichai-Hamburger and McKenna (2006) because the internet essentially "levels the playing field"—anonymity regarding economic status, ethnicity, and religious identification may be maintained and the internet can help reduce stranger anxiety as well. Online participation in a variety of activities can actually reduce anxiety because individuals report feeling more confident in how they verbally describe themselves and show a perception in being better equipped to control and mediate various situations while online. Additionally, many individuals report preferences in building online relationships because it makes them feel "more in control" of events if they do wish to meet others personally. The contact hypothesis argues that individuals are better able to build positive relationships with each other because their perceptions among other group members have improved while working toward their superordinate goal. Through innovations with the internet use, the benefits of the contact hypothesis have been expanded literally worldwide, as individuals become better equipped to work toward mutually beneficial and superordinate goals.

Amichai-Hamburger and McKenna (2006) have identified a sequential process from which anonymous internet use evolves to various forms of positive (i.e., "real-time") face-to-face intergroup contact:

(a) **Text communication only**. Here, the anonymity is highest—little contact with internet users.

---

[3] http://www.internetlivestats.com/internet-users/.

(b) **Text and images** are provided. Here, individuals are capable of physically seeing who their internet partners are via live video images.

(c) **Communication via video and audio.** Here, now internet users not only see who they are interacting with, but can also hear their voices to become better acquainted to understand their partners.

(d) **Fact-to-face interaction.** Similar to research involving the contact hypothesis, face-t-face interaction allows all group members to share their initial experiences, from strictly an internet relationship to now an interactive relationship. Here, mutual effort is shared toward the attainment of beneficial goals within the community, negative stereotypes are debunked, and positive relationships are formed from internet contact (see Fig. 6.1).

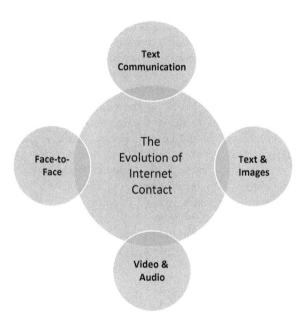

Fig. 6.1 The evolution of internet contact. (Amichai-Hamburger & Katelyn McKenna, 2006)

Establishing Community Resilience via Community Service Activities

Extensive research, both classic (i.e., Sherif and colleagues, 1961) and recent (Ellis & Abdi, 2017), has identified the inherent and unique potential of groups in community development. When provided with opportunities where members may collectively work together and share their skills in community service programs, negative stereotypes reduce and trust significantly increases, thereby reducing the existence of violence and ethnic hate crimes. The interpersonal, social, and psychological benefits of cultures that embrace a more collectivistic approach among community members have been well documented in research (Triandis, 1995; Varnum, Grossman, Kitayama, & Nisbett, 2010). However, an interesting (albeit disturbing) trend that has developed over the last several decades addresses individualistic cultures as expanding globally and how these shifts may be contributing to a more competitive, autonomous, and self-entitled internalized perspective among cultural and community groups (Santos et al. 2017). Expanding global individualistic ideologies and cultures may also contribute to increased polarization among communities and, ultimately, influence (i.e., trigger) more conflict and violence among ethnic and religious groups.

Community members who share a common purpose and sense of connectedness with each other have also shown a greater level of resilience when exposed to different forms of trauma, stress, and natural disasters such as hurricanes and floods (Tidball, Krasny, Svendsen, Campbell, & Helphand, 2010). Additionally, communities that recognize the qualities of collectivistic values are more likely to foster *interdependent* and supportive relationships as an effective process in adapting to trauma and natural or ecologically related disasters (Triandis, 2009). Whether the crisis is a natural disaster such as flooding or hurricanes, or human-related tragedies, we have seen how resilient communities are able to recuperate and the residents rely on each other as viable resources and support systems in the recuperation process.

Tragedy in Las Vegas, NV

Tragically, at the time that this manuscript was being drafted, the single most devastating tragedy unfolded in Las Vegas, NV. On October 1, 2017 the alleged shooter, 64-year-old Stephen Craig Paddock committed the worst mass shooting in modern US history.[4] By the most recent accounts, a total of 59 people were murdered and over 500 injuries were reported by local police. While no known motive is yet to be established for this tragedy, it is becoming increasingly evident that ours is a world that is becoming increasingly vulnerable to the irrational behaviors of individuals (and groups) who attempt to inflict violence to groups based on ethnicity, religion, sexual identity, and political views. It is also becoming increasingly evident that collectively we need to organize our communities in such a way that hatred and fear are replaced with an inherent belief system that individuals can share different ideologies without inflicting hatred on others.

A central theme throughout this text has been the role of community development and the creation of partnerships as key components in helping to build a number of positive attributes, including increased resilience, social connections with community members, and perhaps, most importantly, an ability to understand people through a different lens that promotes equity and social justice. Ethnic conflict, extremism, and violence are problems that have existed for centuries within groups and communities, and have been fueled through the perpetuation of negative stereotypes, stigmas, and the gradual development of silos and polarized communities based on a variety of factors, including religion, economics, ethnicity, and race. Many individuals have argued that these antagonistic traits are indeed inherent, and that humans are biologically predisposed toward conflict and violence. In our earlier review of Jean Jacques Rousseau's analysis of the *social contract*, we discussed how human nature may be predisposed toward conflict when communities and societies do not provide some forum of a democratically determined governance system, whereby individuals are capable of engaging in a collaborative form of dialogue and interaction. John Locke and Rousseau both agreed that while human nature tends to engage in egoistic and opportunistic behaviors, we do have the capacity to live cooperatively and rationally under the rule of law when governing systems are equitable and perceived to serve the best interests of society. Conversely, a weak or corrupt governing system or constitution tends to promote civil unrest and anarchy due to a lack of equity and shared resources. In sum, the basic philosophy of human nature as described by the British empiricists suggests that the human capacity to live within political order rests on our ability to agree on a set of rules that are both fair and equitable to all persons of society. An interactive community structure that provides opportunities of engagement and equitable governance is essential in achieving healthy

[4] https://en.wikipedia.org/wiki/2017_Las_Vegas_Strip_shooting.

community development. These opportunities of engagement afforded to all residents within the community itself then are the primary factors necessary in promoting a resilient and healthy environment for all persons to share and experience.

Communities that provide extended opportunities for individuals to communicate, interact, and share skills with one another through the process of social connection will help increase resiliency and promote understanding of diverse ethnic groups. Perhaps a more important theme that is relevant to the overall thesis of this manuscript is that community growth, development, and resilience are central factors that not only promote resilience and health to each member, but will facilitate growth and understanding, which ultimately reduces the conflict and violence that are increasing today. Community members need to be provided with opportunities to engage with each other and create partnerships as a means of establishing trust and building social capital. Ananthi Al Ramiah and Miles Hewstone (2013) have argued that the key to reducing extremism, ethnic conflict, and violence is first through group contact and also through the formation and development of superordinate goals—the kinds of goals that have the potential to provide benefits to all community members.

Building a More Peaceful Society: Is It Really Possible?

The answer to the question of building a more peaceful society clearly is *yes*. Community service activities, volunteer programs, and community development processes provide individuals with unique opportunities to share their skills and work more collectively and cooperatively with each other. As de Toqueville (1835/2000) has noted, volunteer programs help shape the basic core values of democracy within society by an awareness of the various traits and skills people possess that help build communities. People actually want to contribute to their communities when they feel that their work is valued and it becomes integrated within the process of community growth and development. As we increase our exposure in working with diverse groups within a community, we develop a greater understanding of the unique needs that each person represents. A true sense of "community connectedness" and social capital develops as people feel needed and experience a sense of belonging to their community. Recognizing and identifying the numerous inherent skills that diverse groups possess can build stronger communities as well as a sense of community pride. Similarly, collaborative and interdependent group work that utilizes individual skills and aptitudes creates a bond of trust that promotes social capital and actually increases the resilience and strength within the community itself.

In short, communities provide the fabric in which we learn to live with one another through the development and achievement of mutually beneficial (i.e., superordinate) goals. The more complicated question, however, is, if we as a society are prepared to begin our work proactively and to take the responsibility in providing communities with the tools and resources to do so and make our society and community more interactive, cooperative, and, ultimately, more peaceful? As Staub (2013) indicates, building a more peaceful society or community *starts* with teaching individuals (i.e., children) to learn to develop a more positive and favorable perception of those individuals who historically have been viewed as antagonistic or reprehensible. A more peaceful society and community also begins with a culture that understands that extreme violence and hatred are not biologically inherent characteristics, but rather consequences of harsh economic factors inflicted typically under an authoritarian regime. Tolerant, respectful, and civil behaviors are learned through proactive stewardship principles that are displayed throughout the community—in schools, recreational parks, and within the home. Additionally, we have learned that the antithesis of gratuitous violence that is directed toward underrepresented groups, ethnic conflict, and hate crimes are reduced and eliminated when they are confronted by a conscientious and socially responsible community.

As Staub (2013) discusses in his own research, a more peaceful, civilized, and respectful community can only exist when we reduce inherent polarizing tendencies that we all share (i.e., "us versus them" or the "zero-sum" approach that is common among individualistic cultures) and develop a more interactive, cooperative, and socially responsible approach to human coexistence. Extended or "deep" contact, development of collaborative community growth projects, and superordinate goals are highly effective in promoting more positive relationships with groups that have previously been considered unapproachable or anathema. Even those groups that have remained diametrically opposed from one another for centuries, such as the Palestinians and Israelis, have been shown to increase levels of empathy and humanitarian concerns for one another after being exposed to structured group activities that provided opportunities for interpersonal growth and development. The human capacity in developing a more prosocial and empathic interaction is essentially dependent on the development of cooperative relationships, intergroup contact, and superordinate goals. Perhaps most importantly, as a community, we need to remember that humans, despite the propensity toward violence, have the capacity to change and engage in more meaningful, interactive, and humanistic contact with others.

BUILDING PEACE: A TIME AND PLACE FOR RECONCILIATION, ACCEPTANCE, AND FORGIVENESS

Staub (2013) also identifies the inherent value of the practices of "prevention and reconciliation" (p. 582)—an awareness and acknowledgment of the conflict that innocent individuals have experienced, but also the need to develop personal fortitude in *accepting* these travesties and injustices. The development of reconciliation among groups that historically have had conflicted relationships with each other (i.e., Israelis and Palestinians) will provide the opportunity for a "peaceful coexistence" with each other. Recent research yields encouraging results addressing clashes among ethnic groups that have had a history (i.e., centuries) of conflict with each other.

A predominant theme throughout this manuscript has focused on the need for historically polarized groups to first establish some form of contact (i.e., interactive community service work activities) with each other and then identify mutually beneficial goals that will be shared by all group members. Cehajic, Brown, and Castano (2008) have also identified two key factors in improving relationships among groups that have traditionally experienced conflict with each other: *positive intergroup contact* and *strong in-group identification* (i.e., the realization of common values). Increased contact and exposure among traditionally polarized groups will help each discover the similarities that they, in fact, do share with one another, and perhaps more importantly, will provide opportunities for recognizing transgressions against each group and lead to a greater form of in-group reconciliation (Brown & Hewstone, 2005). In their research addressing the powerful impact of intergroup contact and common in-group identification, Cehajic and colleagues (2008) identified the positive effects of intergroup contact among Bosnian Muslims and Serbs during the 1992 war in Herzegovina. The researchers found that an essential factor to improving intergroup contact and positive interaction was through the development of *empathy* between the groups, which ultimately provided the capacity for forgiveness. It appears that understanding (and appreciating) the life hardships that individuals may experience is a contributing factor to the first steps in communication and engagement with traditionally diametrically opposed groups.

In order for conflict to be truly understood, reduced, and (hopefully) eliminated, there is the need for an objective and impartial understanding of human behavior through the lens of culture. As Sternberg (2017) indicates, society's failure to consider the overwhelming importance and ramification of culture is certainly not cost free, but in fact both detrimental and quite costly. Various cultures throughout the world (i.e., individualistic and collectivistic, etc.) define and shape our behaviors and can often justify even the most violent and egregious conflicts. Only through increased contact and a realization of the need for both sides to work together collaboratively can long-standing feuds, polarizing ideologies perpetuated through extremist practices, and ethnic conflict be resolved to achieve a truly more civil, harmonious, and peaceful society.

REFERENCES

Agani, F., Landau, J., & Agani, N. (2010). Community-building before, during, and after times of trauma: The application of the LINC model of community resilience in Kosovo. *American Journal of Orthopsychiatry, 80*(1), 143–149.

Al Ramiah, A., & Hewstone, M. (2013). Intergroup contact as a tool for reducing, resolving, and preventing intergroup conflict. *American Psychologist, 68*(7), 527–542.

Amichai-Hamburger, Y., & McKenna, K. Y. A. (2006). The contact hypothesis reconsidered: Interacting via the internet. *Journal of Computer-Mediated Communication, 11*, 825–843.

Brown, R., & Hewstone, M. (2005). An integrative theory of intergroup contact. *Advances in Experimental and Social Psychology, 37*, 255–343.

Cehajic, S., Brown, R., & Castano, E. (2008). Forgive and forget? Antecedents and consequences of intergroup forgiveness in Bosnia and Herzegovina. *Political Psychology, 29*(3), 351–367.

De Tocqueville, A. (2000). *Democracy in America* (H. C. Mansfield & D. Winthrop, Trans.). Chicago: University of Chicago Press. (Original work published in 1835).

Ellis, B. H., & Abdi, S. (2011). *Media reporting and Somali youth perspectives* [Unpublished data]. Boston, MA: Boston Children's Hospital.

Ellis, B. H., & Abdi, S. (2017). Building community resilience to violent extremism through genuine partnerships. *American Psychologist, 72*(3), 289–300.

Gaertner, S. L., Dovidio, J. F., Banker, B. S., Houlette, M., Johnson, K. M., & McGlynn, E. A. (2000). Reducing intergroup conflict: From superordinate goals to decategorization, recategorization, and mutual differentiation. *Group Dynamics: Theory, Research and Practice*, 4(1), 98–114.

Gaertner, S. L., Mann, J. A., Murrell, A. J., & Dovidio, J. F. (1989). Reduction of intergroup bias: The benefits of recategorization. *Journal of Personality and Social Psychology*, 57, 239–249.

Glover, T. D., Shinew, K. J., & Parry, D. C. (2005). Association, sociability, and civic culture: The democratic effect of community gardening. *Leisure Sciences*, 27, 75–92.

Hobbes, T. (1651). *Leviathon*. Oxford University Press.

Locke, J. (2003). *Two Treatises of government and a letter concerning toleration*. New Haven: Yale University Press.

McClendon, M. J. (1974). Interracial contact and the reduction of prejudice. *Sociological Focus*, 7(4), 47–65.

Miller, E. (2014). *Patterns of terrorism in the United States, 1970–2013: Final report to Resilient Systems Division, DHS Science and Technology Directorate*. College Park, MD: START.

Peterson, L. E., & Dietz, J. (2005). Enforcement of workforce homogeneity and prejudice as explanations for employment discrimination. *Journal of Applied Social Psychology*, 35, 144–159.

Pettigrew, T. F., & Tropp, L. R. (2006). A meta-analytic test of intergroup contact theory. *Journal of Personality and Social Psychology*, 90, 751–783.

Ridge, R. D., & Montoya, J. A. (2013). Favorable contact during volunteer service: Reducing prejudice toward Mexicans in the American Southwest. *Journal of Community & Applied Social Psychology*, 23, 466–480.

Riley, K. A. (2013). Walking the leadership tightrope: Building community cohesiveness and social capital in schools in highly disadvantaged urban communities. *British Education Research Journal*, 39(2), 266–286.

Rousseau, J. J. (1762). *The social contract, or principles of the political right*. http://ebooks.adelaide.edu.au/r/rousseau/jean_jacques/r864s/.

Saab, R., Harb, C., & Moughalian, C. (2017). Intergroup contact as a predictor of violent and nonviolent collective action: Evidence from Syrian refugees and Lebanese Nationals. *Peace and Conflict: Journal of Peace Psychology*, 23(3), 297–306.

Santos, H. C., Varnum, M. E. W., & Grossman, I. (2017). Global increases in individualism. *Psychological Science*, 28(9), 1228–1239.

Sherif, M., Harvey, O. J., White, B. J., Hood, W. R., & Sherif, C. W. (1961). *Intergroup conflict and cooperation: The Robber's Cave Experiment*. Norman: University of Oklahoma Book Exchange.

Sidanious, J., & Pratto, F. (1999). *Social dominance: An intergroup theory of social hierarchy and oppression*. Cambridge, UK: Cambridge University Press.

Staub, E. (2013). Building a peaceful society: Origins, prevention, and reconciliation after genocide and other group violence. *American Psychologist, 68*(7), 576–589.

Sternberg, R. (2017). Some lessons from a symposium on cultural psychological science. *Psychological Science, 12*(5), 911–921.

Tidball, K. G., Krasny, M. E., Svendsen, E., Campbell, L., & Helphand, K. (2010). Stewardship, learning, and memory in disaster resilience. *Environmental Education Research, 16*(5–6), 591–609.

Triandis, H. C. (1995). *Individualism and collectivism: New directions in social psychology.* Boulder, CO: Westview Press.

Triandis, H. C. (2009). Ecological determinants of cultural variations. In R. S. Wyer, C. Chiu, Y. Hong, & D. Cohen (Eds.), *Understanding culture: Theory, research and applications* (pp. 189–210). New York, NY: Psychological Press.

Umphress, E. E., Smith-Crowe, K., Brief, A. P., Dietz, J., & Baskerville-Watkins, M. (2007). When birds of a feather flock together and when they do not: Status composition, social dominance orientation, and organizational attractiveness. *Journal of Applied Psychology, 92*(2), 396–409.

Varnum, M. E. W., Grossmann, I., Kitayama, S., & Nisbett, R. E. (2010). The origin of cultural differences in cognition: Evidence of the social orientation hypothesis. *Current Directions in Psychological Science, 19*, 9–13.

CHAPTER 7

Concluding Notes: The Virtues of Hope

> Let the Heavens rejoice, Let the Earth be glad … Let the Sea
> resound, and all that is in it. Let the Fields be jubilant, and
> everything in them … Let all of the Forest sing for Joy.
> *Psalm, 96:11–12*

In our efforts to rebuild communities that are more inclusive and equitable, we need to remind ourselves of the positive effects of group work and how distinct environments (i.e., "green spaces" and community gardens, forests, etc.) can help influence a greater degree of community unity, connectedness, and self-worth. Our own evolutionary history has shown us that nature has both calming and healing effects when we begin work from an interactive and cooperative perspective. In this sense, then, we are both stewards of the community and tenants of the Earth in providing a healthy environment in which we all share. Continuous themes addressed throughout this manuscript involve extremism, violence, and the unique role that communities have in helping groups of individuals realize their potential and work within a more constructive and cohesive process that brings them together. Exposure to specific types of environments (i.e., "green spaces," community gardens, and urban forestry programs) has been identified as key elements in promoting mental (and physical) health

© The Author(s) 2018
A. J. Hoffman et al., *The Role of Community Development
in Reducing Extremism and Ethnic Conflict*,
https://Doi.org/10.1007/978-3-319-75699-8_7

benefits, such as reduced stress and anxiety as well as improved sociability and civic ideologies that foster and promote interactive and democratic processes in community development (Glover, Shinew, & Parry, 2005).

Interestingly, even specific types of negative environmental auditory stimulation (i.e., "noise") have been identified as contributing to frustration, irritability, and cognitive deficits (i.e., delayed language development) among infants and children (Erickson & Newman, 2017).

Perhaps one suggested area of future research can involve addressing the community benefits of exposure to sounds typically found in natural (i.e., "green space") environments. If chronic exposure to negative auditory stimulation has been associated with frustration and interpersonal conflict, perhaps communities and neighborhoods can reduce some of these problems by providing greater access to green space (i.e., community gardens, urban forests, and horticultural programs) environments. Reducing ethnic violence and conflict begins when all groups realize their common core values and similarities with each other while simultaneously reducing negative stereotypes that fuel anger and hatred.

How then can we as a community move beyond the negative rhetoric that impacts us seemingly on a daily basis? The violence that confronts our local and global communities seems to be increasing on a weekly (if not daily) basis and our country appears more divided than ever in agreeing what approaches should be used to counter these conflicts and how to begin the healing process. At the time this manuscript was being drafted, on the evening of Sunday, October 1, 2017, the single greatest massacre (i.e., mass shooting) in US history occurred in Las Vegas, NV. The assailant (Stephen Paddock) fired literally thousands of live ammo rounds from his window from the Mandalay Bay Hotel into the crowds of the Route 91 Harvest music festival located on the Las Vegas Strip. At first many concert goers reported that they thought the sounds were "fireworks going off," but when they realized an active shooting was unfolding, pandemonium followed. One Las Vegas cab driver picked up as many injured people in her cab as she could and drove them to safety, while the majority of the security guards who were working that evening stayed to help coordinate with the frantic people trying to escape the mayhem. One security guard (Jesus Campos) was named "an absolute hero" by the media (*Las Vegas Sun*, October 9, 2017) for alerting the law enforcement authorities to the specific location of the gunman despite being shot in the leg.[1] While catastrophes and disasters can be horrific to experience, in many situations, how humans respond to their communities in crisis reflects a selfless and altruistic behavior that represents the essence of true heroism.

The underlying theme in overcoming violence and conflict is through an awareness and realization that human behavior, despite the extreme negativism that we see all too often through the media, is in fact capable of positive change and growth. Perhaps a greater sense of empathic concern and ability to experience the plight and suffering of others may yield a community that is more likely to intervene and help others when necessary. Simply stated, we are more likely to intervene and help others when we show a greater capacity to understand (and in some cases even experience) the psychological (and physical) pain that out-group members may be experiencing (Batson, Bolen, Cross, & Neuringer-Benefiel, 1986). We are not only capable of "tolerating" our differences, we are both psychologically (Edwards, Jones, Mitchell, Hagler, & Roberts, 2016) and evolutionarily (Axelrod, 1984) well equipped to create a more cooperative community that helps all persons identify a stronger sense of identity and "community connectedness," which ultimately is essential in reducing conflict.

While the trauma and horror from the October 1, 2017 shooting (and other shooting tragedies) remain tragic in American history, perhaps one positive outgrowth from this event was the heroism that existed among people saving lives that day. Perhaps the most important statement or message offered throughout this manuscript is that *all* groups, regardless of ethnicity, religion, gender, or sex, have the capacity to live and coexist in peace. The true virtue of hope, then, is the inherent belief that life circumstances can and will change for the better, no matter how bleak our futures may appear at the current moment. The virtues of hope, forgiveness, and community stewardship are essential in any effort to help reduce ethnic conflict and violence, as they are the cornerstone and foundation of a strong and resilient society.

A peaceful society begins with the recognition that all residents within society have skills and potential that provide the foundation in building a stronger and more resilient community. The development of community prevention programs that provide opportunities for individuals to work collaboratively to attain mutually beneficial (superordinate) goals can

---

[1] https://patch.com/nevada/lasvegas/guards-heroes-vegas-shooting-our-people-they-didnt-run.

establish both an improved understanding of one another and interdependency within the group itself. Schools and communities can provide opportunities for community members to work collaboratively in providing healthier foods (i.e., "green" ecologically sustainable community gardens and fruit tree orchards) to low-income residents (see Fig. 7.1). Community growth and development can only occur when residents are provided opportunities to share experiences and understand and learn from one another. A contributing factor to conflict, aggression, and hate crimes is a

Fig. 7.1 Community Participatory Student Cooperative: Inver Hills—Metropolitan State University Community Garden (August 2017)

lack of preventative community development projects that provide opportunities of growth and understanding that dispel negative stereotypes known to trigger violence.

The development of cooperative groups and community service programs helps reduce violence and conflict because such programs decrease polarization, increase contact among out-group and in-group members, and help debunk the negative myths and stereotypes that often fuel hatred and misunderstanding (Gaertner et al., 2000). Humans have *both* a biological and an evolutionary need to not only coexist with each other, but to contribute to a stronger and more resilient community (Allen-Arave, Guren, & Hill, 2008; Hoffman, 2015). When community residents and children are provided with the basic ingredients (i.e., social competence) of a healthy community, then that community becomes less violent and more empowered (Flannery et al., 2003). Reducing extremism, racial conflict, and genocide is a goal that is both realistic and viable only when we provide individuals with the opportunities to discover their strengths *with* each other, not *against* each other.

The first step in building a peaceful society begins with communities that recognize that all persons have the potential to contribute to a stronger and more resilient society. A proactive community develops programs that facilitate the interactive and communicative process with new immigrants and current residents. A proactive community is one that welcomes everyone and shares its resources while establishing trust among all residents. Finally, traditional human behaviors that have remained problematic (i.e., ethnic violence and extremism) are, in fact, capable of change only if we invest and capitalize in the inherent strengths that exist in all community residents.

REFERENCES

Allen-Arave, W., Gurven, M., & Hill, K. (2008). Reciprocal altruism, rather than kin selection, maintains nepotistic food transfers on an Ache reservation. *Evolution and Human Behavior, 29*, 305–318.

Axelrod, R. (1984). *The evolution of cooperation*. New York: Basic Books.

Batson, C. D., Bolen, M. H., Cross, J. A., & Neuringer-Benefiel, H. E. (1986). Where is the altruism in the altruistic personality? *Journal of Personality and Social Psychology, 50*(1), 212–220.

Edwards, K. M., Jones, L. M., Mitchell, K. J., Hagler, M. A., & Roberts, L. T. (2016). Building on youth's strengths: A call to include adolescents in developing, implementing, and evaluating violence prevention programs. *Psychology of Violence, 6*(1), 15–21.

Erickson, L., & Newman, R. S. (2017). Influences of background noise on infants and children. *Current Directions in Psychological Science, 26*(5), 451–457.

Flannery, D. J., Vazsonyi, A. T., Liau, A. K., Guo, S., Powell, K. E., Atha, H., Vesterdal, W., & Embry, D. (2003). Initial behavior outcomes for the Peacebuilders universal school-based violence prevention program. *Developmental Psychology, 39*(2), 292–308.

Gaertner, S. L., Dovidio, J. F., Banker, B. S., Houlette, M., Johnson, K. M., & McGlynn, E. A. (2000). Reducing intergroup conflict: From superordinate goals to decategorization, recategorization, and mutual differentiation. *Group Dynamics: Theory, Research and Practice, 4*(1), 98–114.

Glover, T. D., Shinew, K. J., & Parry, D. C. (2005). Association, sociability, and civic culture: The Democratic effect of community gardening. *Leisure Sciences, 27*, 75–92.

Hoffman, A. J. (2015). Community service work and the virtues of apple trees: Planting seeds of hope in the Newtown victory garden. *Global Journal of Community Psychology Practice, 6*(1), 1–12.

Index[1]

---

[1] Note: Page numbers followed by 'n' refer to notes.

© The Author(s) 2018
A. J. Hoffman et al., *The Role of Community Development in Reducing Extremism and Ethnic Conflict*,
https://doi.org/10.1007/978-3-319-75699-8

CPSIA information can be obtained
at www.ICGtesting.com
Printed in the USA
LVHW062358040619
620112LV00005B/83/P